NICK SHAW

Fortune in a Weekend: Launch Your 7 Figure Business in 48 Hours

Copyright © 2024 by Nick Shaw

All rights reserved. No part of this publication may be reproduced, stored or transmitted in any form or by any means, electronic, mechanical, photocopying, recording, scanning, or otherwise without written permission from the publisher. It is illegal to copy this book, post it to a website, or distribute it by any other means without permission.

First edition

This book was professionally typeset on Reedsy.
Find out more at reedsy.com

Contents

Introduction	1
Chapter 1: The Million Dollar Mindset	4
Embrace the Entrepreneurial Spirit	4
Overcoming Fear and Doubt	7
Chapter 2: The Power of the Weekend	10
Why 48 Hours Is All You Need	10
Real-Life Success Stories	13
Chapter 3: Brainstorming the Right Idea	17
Identifying Market Gaps	17
Validating Your Ideas Quickly	20
Chapter 4: Research and Preparation	24
Knowing Your Audience	24
Analyzing the Competition	27
Chapter 5: Setting Up Shop	30
Choosing a Business Model	30
Creating a Business Plan	33
Chapter 6: Funding Your Business	36
Bootstrapping Basics	36
Alternative Financing Options	39
Chapter 7: Legal and Administrative Set-Up	43
Business Structure and Registration	43
Essential Legal Considerations	46
Chapter 8: Building Your Brand	50
Crafting Your Brand Identity	50
Designing a Logo and Tagline	53
Chapter 9: Creating a Website	56

Choosing a Domain Name	56
Building and Launching Your Site	59
Chapter 10: Social Media Presence	62
Setting Up Key Platforms	62
Engaging Your Audience	65
Chapter 11: Product Development	69
Prototyping Quickly	69
Iterating Based on Feedback	72
Chapter 12: Pricing Strategies	75
Calculating Costs and Margins	75
Establishing Competitive Prices	78
Chapter 13: Marketing and Sales Plan	82
Crafting Your Message	82
Choosing Marketing Channels	85
Chapter 14: Launch Day Strategy	88
Preparing for Launch	88
Executing the Launch	91
Chapter 15: Customer Acquisition	95
Lead Generation Techniques	95
Converting Leads to Customers	98
Chapter 16: Scaling Your Operations	101
Streamlining Processes	101
Hiring and Outsourcing	104
Chapter 17: Financial Management	107
Budgeting and Forecasting	107
Tax Considerations	110
Chapter 18: Customer Retention	114
Building Loyalty Programs	114
Creating Exceptional Customer Service	117
Chapter 19: Leveraging Technology	121
Essential Tools and Software	121
Automation and Efficiency	124
Chapter 20: Building a Strong Team	128

Recruiting Talent	128
Team Dynamics and Leadership	131
Chapter 21: Continuous Improvement	134
Analyzing Performance	134
Adapting to Market Changes	137
Chapter 22: Managing Stress and Burnout	141
Work-Life Balance Tips	141
Mental Health Resources	144
Chapter 23: Networking and Partnerships	147
Building Strategic Relationships	147
Collaborating for Success	150
Chapter 24: Case Studies of Weekend Success	153
Real Stories and Lessons Learned	153
Common Pitfalls and How to Avoid Them	156
Chapter 25: The Road Ahead	160
Setting Long-Term Goals	160
Planning for Sustainable Growth	163
Conclusion	167
Appendix A: Resources and Tools	170
Recommended Books and Websites	170

Introduction

Think about the transformative potential of having a million-dollar business crafted and ready to roll within just 48 hours. Sounds like a stretch, doesn't it? Well, stick around, and you'll discover that it's entirely possible—and surprisingly practical. This book is here to challenge your preconceived notions about entrepreneurship and side hustles. It's designed to help you jumpstart a venture that could very well change your life in ways you never imagined.

Our fast-paced world demands innovative strategies for making the most out of limited time. And yes, you can absolutely build something monumental over a weekend. This book is not just about breaking down barriers; it's about shattering them with a hammer of focus, strategy, and action. Whether you're a stay-at-home mom balancing kids and passions, a student looking for a way to pay tuition without sacrificing study time, or a seasoned entrepreneur looking to add another feather to your cap, this guide has got you covered.

Let's be clear—starting a million-dollar business isn't about shortcuts, but about smart cuts. It's not so much about bypassing hard work but rather about focusing your effort so intensely that results come quicker than you ever thought possible. You're going to learn how to leverage the power of a single weekend to do what others might take months, even years, to accomplish.

To begin with, you'll need to adopt a unique mindset—a million-dollar mindset. This isn't just motivational mumbo jumbo; it's about rewiring your thinking to embrace the entrepreneurial spirit that sees opportunities where others see obstacles. Every chapter of this book will guide you through specific strategies and actions that will not only help you build your business swiftly but also set the foundation for long-term success.

You'll delve into practical aspects of idea generation, market research, and product development—all tailored to a rapid timeline. Further, we'll guide you through the intricate details of setting up legal structures, designing a brand, building a website, and launching a powerful marketing plan—all in a manner that prioritizes speed and efficiency. Yes, it's a lot to take in, and yes, it's completely doable.

The role of preparation, research, and quick validation of ideas can't be understated. You'll learn how to dissect market gaps and seize opportunities others have overlooked. We'll explore the significance of validating your idea swiftly, ensuring you're not just running with any concept but one with real potential. This isn't just theoretical knowledge; these are actionable steps you can follow right away.

In subsequent chapters, you'll find detailed insights on various essential functions of a business. From the nitty-gritty of funding your venture through bootstrapping or alternative financing options to the crucial elements of building a robust brand identity—everything is aimed at accelerating your business development cycle.

We'll also touch on modern tools and technologies that can streamline operations, allowing you to maximize output with minimal resources. Automation, efficiency, and smart workforce management will play pivotal roles in your weekend success story. But it's not just about tools and tech; it's also about people. Building a strong team and engaging in effective networking can yield dividends that software solutions alone can't match.

And let's not forget the softer skills. Managing stress, maintaining a work-life balance, and ensuring mental health are crucial, especially when you're pushing limits to achieve extraordinary results. Burnout is a real risk, and this guide ensures you're well-equipped to handle the pressure effectively.

You'll also gain inspiration from real-life success stories of individuals who've turned their weekends into gold mines. Learning from their journeys—their triumphs and pitfalls—can offer invaluable lessons and insights into what works and what doesn't.

As you dive into this process, remember: This isn't just another business

INTRODUCTION

book. It's a road map—a blueprint designed to get you from zero to a million in the shortest time possible. Are you ready to shatter limits, defy expectations, and embark on a journey that could change your life in just two days?

The road ahead is filled with opportunities waiting to be seized. This book will serve as your companion, your toolkit, and your mentor as you navigate this thrilling journey. Get ready to roll up your sleeves and create something phenomenal. Your million-dollar weekend starts now.

Chapter 1: The Million Dollar Mindset

Welcome to the incredible journey of transforming your dreams into a million-dollar reality. The key to success isn't merely having the greatest idea or the most detailed plan; it begins with cultivating the right mindset. To thrive in this fast-paced entrepreneurial world, you must embrace resilience, adaptability, and an insatiable thirst for knowledge. It's about seeing opportunities where others only see obstacles and having the grit to overcome self-doubt and fear. Imagine your mindset as the foundation of a skyscraper; it needs to be robust to support the heights you'll reach. As you step into the realm of rapid wealth creation, remember: your thoughts, attitude, and beliefs will ultimately shape your business's destiny. Let's cultivate that million-dollar mindset together and set the stage for phenomenal success.

Embrace the Entrepreneurial Spirit

In the high-stakes world of business, embracing the entrepreneurial spirit is more than a recommendation; it's an imperative. Success doesn't favor the timid but the bold, the visionaries who dare to see opportunities where others see obstacles. Whether you're a side hustler, a stay-at-home mom, or a 20-something fresh out of college, fostering an entrepreneurial mindset is the cornerstone of transforming your ideas into a million-dollar business. This section will lay the groundwork for developing that transformative mindset, offering insights and practical advice tailored to every aspiring entrepreneur.

First and foremost, understand that the entrepreneurial spirit begins with a mindset shift. It's about pivoting from a mentality of scarcity to one of abundance, from seeing risks to perceiving rewards. Many people make the mistake of thinking that successful entrepreneurs are somehow fundamentally different from them. The truth is, entrepreneurial success is less about innate talent and more about grit, perseverance, and a willingness to learn from failure.

An entrepreneur sees beyond the immediate challenges and focuses on the bigger picture. This involves cultivating a forward-thinking mentality. Ask yourself, "What future possibilities exist within this current challenge?" Use this perspective to generate innovative solutions that will set you apart from the competition. It's a continuous cycle of dreaming, planning, executing, learning, and reiterating.

One of the fundamental characteristics of this spirit is adaptability. The business landscape is ever-changing, and those who can't adapt are quickly left behind. Entrepreneurs who thrive are those who see change and not as a threat but as a chance to innovate. Be prepared to pivot if necessary. Often, the initial idea may not be the one that drives you to success, but a version of it refined through market feedback and real-world application.

Risk-taking is an inherent aspect of entrepreneurship. However, it's not about taking blind risks; it's about calculated risks. There's an art to balancing risk and reward, and mastering this art is critical. Start by conducting thorough research and analysis. Understand your market, identify potential pitfalls, and develop contingency plans. This doesn't eliminate risks, but it mitigates them, allowing you to move forward with confidence.

Having a passion for what you do can be the fuel that drives your entrepreneurial journey. Passion brings energy, and energy can be the difference between giving up when things are tough and pushing through to find a solution. Passion is also contagious; it inspires your team, attracts customers, and can even sway investors. It's your why, and it should be at the core of everything you do.

Networking is another essential element. Building a network of mentors, peers, and industry connections can provide invaluable resources for advice, support, and collaboration. Don't shy away from seeking mentorship; most seasoned entrepreneurs are eager to share their wisdom with those just starting. Your network can also open doors to opportunities you might not have found otherwise.

An often-overlooked aspect is the importance of storytelling. Your ability to tell a compelling story about your brand and your journey can significantly impact your business's success. Stories resonate on an emotional level, helping to forge stronger connections with your audience, whether they are customers, partners, or investors. Craft a narrative that highlights your vision, your journey, and your mission.

Learning to manage fear and doubt is crucial. Fear is natural, but it's how you handle it that determines your success. An entrepreneurial mindset embraces uncertainty and views it as a part of the journey. Surround yourself with positive influences and maintain a balanced perspective. When doubt creeps in, revisit your successes, however small, to remind yourself of your capabilities.

Self-discipline and time management cannot be overstated. With limited time, especially if you're balancing a side hustle with other commitments, every minute counts. Set clear goals and prioritize tasks that align with your long-term vision. Utilize tools and technologies to streamline processes and increase productivity. Remember, it's not about working harder but working smarter.

As you set off on your entrepreneurial journey, remember that innovation doesn't always mean inventing something entirely new. It can mean improving an existing product or service, finding a new way to deliver it, or even targeting a previously overlooked market segment. Innovation is about finding a unique angle that differentiates you from the rest.

Finally, maintain a growth mindset. The world of entrepreneurship is a constant learning curve. View every setback as a learning opportunity and every success as a stepping stone to greater achievements. Stay curious, stay humble, and always be willing to learn and adapt. Continuous improvement isn't just a practice; it's a philosophy.

Embracing the entrepreneurial spirit means setting yourself on a continuous path of personal and professional growth. It's about harnessing your creativity, taking inspired action, and forging ahead despite the odds. Whether you're starting this journey on a bustling weekend or navigating it over months and years, remember that the entrepreneurial spirit is a blend of persistence, innovation, and an unyielding belief in the possibility of turning your dreams into reality.

As we dive deeper into "The Million Dollar Mindset," keep this entrepreneurial spirit at the forefront. Let it guide your decisions, inspire your actions, and give you the courage to take the leap. With this mindset, you're not just starting a business; you're building your future, one decision at a time.

Overcoming Fear and Doubt

Embarking on the journey to launch a million-dollar business in 48 hours isn't for the faint of heart. It's completely natural to feel a surge of fear and doubt. These emotions are part of the entrepreneurial experience, but they must be managed effectively to achieve success. Addressing them head-on can transform obstacles into stepping stones.

First, recognize that fear is not the enemy. It's a natural response to stepping out of your comfort zone. Without fear, we wouldn't have the adrenaline rush that primes us for action. Fear means you are pushing your boundaries, and that's a good thing. Embrace it. Accept that it will walk alongside you, but don't let it hold the reins.

Doubt can be more insidious. It creeps into your thoughts, casting shadows over your plans and ambitions. To combat doubt, start by understanding its source. Often, it stems from a lack of confidence or the magnitude of the task at hand. Break your big goal into smaller, achievable tasks. This makes the journey seem more manageable and less daunting.

Visualization is another potent tool against fear and doubt. Picture your end goal vividly. Imagine the launch day, the first sale, and the moment when your business idea catches fire. See yourself as a successful entrepreneur. Visualization helps to train your mind to focus on positive outcomes rather than potential failures.

When doubt arises, one practical step is to seek out mentors and advisors. They can offer a fresh perspective and advice born from experience. Surrounding yourself with a network of supportive individuals can provide validation and constructive criticism that propels you forward. Connecting with like-minded peers is equally important; their journey can offer insights and communal encouragement.

Remember, mistakes are bound to happen. When they do, view them as learning opportunities. Each error is a lesson in disguise. Analyze what went wrong and take steps to avoid similar pitfalls in the future. This mindset shift—from fearing mistakes to embracing them—can reduce doubt significantly.

Set realistic expectations to balance your enthusiasm. It's easy to let your imagination run wild with visions of overnight success, but understand that real progress takes time. Prepare yourself mentally and emotionally for potential setbacks. Managing expectations can mitigate the impact of unforeseen challenges, keeping you steady and focused.

Time management is crucial. Working against the clock can induce fear if you feel unprepared. A detailed plan outlining each step you need to take within those 48 hours can provide clarity and direction. Allocate specific time blocks for brainstorming, market research, setting up your website, and initial marketing efforts. Stick to your schedule as closely as possible to maintain momentum.

Practicing mindfulness and stress-relief techniques can also be advantageous. Meditation, deep-breathing exercises, and even brief moments of calm can help keep fear and doubt at bay. A clear, focused mind is more resilient to stress and better equipped to handle unexpected obstacles.

It helps to remind yourself why you decided to take this leap in the first place. Reconnect with your underlying motivation and passion. Whether it's financial independence, creative fulfillment, or making a positive impact, anchor yourself in that purpose. Your why can serve as your north star, guiding you through moments of uncertainty.

Additionally, affirmations and positive self-talk can effectively counteract doubt. Replace negative thoughts with empowering statements. Instead of thinking, "I can't do this," remind yourself, "I have the skills and determination to succeed." Over time, this shift in internal dialogue can boost your confidence.

Sometimes, it's essential to take a step back and recalibrate. If you feel overwhelmed, give yourself a brief break. A short walk, a talk with a loved one, or even a quick distraction can reset your mental state. Returning with a fresh perspective can often illuminate solutions you hadn't considered before.

Fear and doubt can also be tempered by gaining knowledge and skills. The more you learn about your market, your potential customers, and the mechanics of setting up a business, the more confident you'll become. Knowledge begets confidence, and confidence diminishes doubt.

Empathy can be surprisingly powerful as well. Put yourself in your customers' shoes. Understanding their problems and how your business can solve them can shift your focus from internal fears to external, actionable goals. When your mission is to help others, fear and doubt often take a back seat.

Finally, celebrate your small wins. Each step you take, no matter how minor it seems, is progress. Recognize and appreciate these accomplishments. They serve as constant reminders of your capability and resilience.

Remember, everyone who has ever achieved something great faced fear and doubt. It's overcoming these feelings that sets successful entrepreneurs apart from the rest. Harness that energy, use the strategies mentioned, and transform your mindset into one that thrives on challenges and exudes confidence. You are on the path to creating something extraordinary.

Chapter 2: The Power of the Weekend

It's easy to underestimate the potential locked within a mere 48 hours, but the weekend offers an unparalleled opportunity to ignite your entrepreneurial journey. When you focus intensely on a well-structured plan, these two days can become a catalyst for incredible transformation. Think about it: no distractions from the usual workweek hustle, just pure, undivided attention on building something tangible. By harnessing this time, you can brainstorm ideas, set up key operations, and even make your first sale before Monday dawns. The weekend is more than just a break from routine—it's a powerful incubator where million-dollar ventures are born and nurtured. Use these 48 hours wisely, and watch how small, deliberate actions can generate immense momentum for your business aspirations.

Why 48 Hours Is All You Need

When most people think of starting a million-dollar business, their minds flood with images of long nights, years of toil, and a sacrifice-laden journey. But what if you could kickstart that dream over a weekend? Believe it or not, 48 hours is all you need to lay down the foundations for a successful business. This brief but intensely focused time frame forces you to leverage two powerful assets: concentrated effort and the urgency of a tight deadline. Together, these can work wonders.

Consider the weekend as a pressure cooker for productivity. The time constraint compels you to prioritize your tasks down to the minutiae. You can't afford to fiddle with non-essentials. This stringent focus allows you

CHAPTER 2: THE POWER OF THE WEEKEND

to eliminate wasteful activities and concentrate solely on actions that propel your business idea forward. When you're under the gun, there's no room for overthinking or second-guessing. You move with purpose and clarity.

The beauty of this compressed timeframe is that it levels the playing field. Whether you're a student, a stay-at-home parent, or someone juggling a full-time job, anyone can carve out a weekend to devote to their entrepreneurial dreams. This democratization of time removes barriers that often discourage people from starting something new. It's not about finding months or years; it's about carving out two days to make a concerted effort. That's a manageable investment with potentially transformative returns.

Distractions are the nemesis of productivity. Imagine how much you could accomplish if you blocked out all distractions for just 48 hours. No social media, no Netflix, no trivial errands—just undiluted focus on your business idea. The weekend's natural structure also supports this. With the typical weekday routines temporarily paused, you have a clean slate to work on something that could change your life.

Psychologically speaking, knowing you have only 48 hours triggers a heightened sense of urgency. Similar to how students often pull off miraculous all-nighters before exams, a concentrated weekend effort can yield astounding results. This psychological urgency translates into physical momentum—entropy turns into energy, and idle thoughts become actionable tasks. It's this kinetic energy that fuels breakthroughs and innovation.

Fast decision-making becomes a necessity rather than an afterthought. In a 48-hour sprint, you don't have the luxury to ponder every option endlessly. Instead, you learn to trust your instincts and make quick but informed decisions. This decisiveness is a crucial entrepreneurial trait. Most successful entrepreneurs will tell you that action beats indecision any day. A calculated, quick decision made today is far more productive than a perfect decision made months later.

Moreover, the limited time frame encourages efficiency. With only two days on the clock, you're more inclined to leverage tools and resources that accelerate your progress. Whether it's adopting pre-made templates for business plans, using website builders that require zero coding knowledge, or tapping into freelance marketplaces for quick logo designs, the emphasis is on getting things done quickly and effectively. This focus on efficiency can carry over into the later stages of your business development, continuously streamlining your operations.

Another key advantage of this rapid approach is that it forces you to validate your business ideas quickly. Instead of spending weeks or months developing a product or service only to discover there's no market for it, you can test your concept almost immediately. This rapid validation process can save you considerable time, money, and emotional investment. By getting immediate feedback, you can pivot, refine, or even abandon an idea without the prolonged agony of wondering if it will ever catch on.

In this 48-hour period, your commitment levels soar. When you know you have a limited amount of time, you're more likely to be fully committed to the task at hand. You're not just dipping a toe in the water; you're diving in headfirst. This kind of immersion fosters a deeper connection to your business idea and propels you into a state of flow—a mental state where productivity and creativity are at their peak.

This approach also cultivates resilience. Condensing the start of a business into a weekend can be demanding, and things won't always go as planned. But facing and overcoming these challenges in quick succession builds resilience. You learn to adapt, to course-correct, and to handle pressure—all invaluable skills for any entrepreneur. The concentrated experience prepares you for the unpredictable nature of running a business.

The importance of a strong support network can't be understated in this context. By informing friends, family, or even mentors about your 48-hour business sprint, you create a network of accountability. Their encouragement and interest can serve as additional motivation to keep you pushing through the inevitable challenges. Accountability is a powerful motivator, and knowing that others are watching can drive you to achieve remarkable things.

There's also an element of excitement and novelty in launching a business over a weekend. The compressed timeline adds a layer of adrenaline to the process, making it not just a project, but an adventure. This intrigue can keep you engaged and driven, unlike prolonged projects that can fizzle out due to loss of interest or fatigue. The sense of accomplishment and exhilaration at the end of those 48 hours are immense, rewarding you for your dedication and hard work.

Many people have produced extraordinary results under extreme time constraints. Think about hackathons, where teams develop functioning prototypes of software in just 24-48 hours. These events have given rise to startups, innovations, and even major tech acquisitions. The concentrated effort brings out the best in people, proving once again that limited time can be a catalyst for unlimited possibilities.

By setting ambitious but achievable goals for your weekend, you create a clear roadmap for success. Whether it's validating a business idea, launching a website, or making your first sales, these tangible milestones provide you with direction and focus. Every task accomplished serves as a building block, propelling you closer to your ultimate objective. This momentum is crucial; each small victory fuels your drive to achieve the next.

In conclusion, the magic of a 48-hour business launch lies in its ability to concentrate your efforts, create urgency, and channel your focus. It makes the daunting task of starting a business feel manageable and achievable. You won't just lay the groundwork; you'll establish a solid foundation upon which to build your million-dollar venture. It's proof that with right mindset, preparation, and determination, two days can indeed be all you need to set your entrepreneurial dreams in motion.

Real-Life Success Stories

The commendable power of a mere 48 hours can transform a simple idea scribbled on a napkin into a thriving, revenue-generating business. Let's delve into some inspiring real-life success stories that vividly illustrate the impact of the weekend hustle.

Take Sarah, for example. She was a stay-at-home mom with a knack for baking. Troubled by mounting bills and seeking an additional income stream, she decided to turn her passion into a business. Over one weekend, Sarah gathered her best recipes, baked samples, and created a website with an easy-to-use order form. By Sunday night, her social media pages were buzzing with orders. She partnered with a local coffee shop to provide freshly baked goods each morning. Within months, her side hustle flourished into a full-fledged bakery, earning her six figures annually.

Another standout story is that of Jason, a college student studying computer science. Fascinated by the complexities of blockchain technology, he envisioned a platform where people could trade digital assets securely. Allocating his weekend purely to this idea, he joined forces with friends who had complementary skills. They developed a minimalist prototype and garnered initial users by posting on niche forums and Reddit. Today, his platform has secured millions in venture capital funding and positioned itself as a reputable player in the fintech community.

Many entrepreneurs find themselves constrained by weekday responsibilities. It's worth noting that the weekend affords a unique opportunity for deep, uninterrupted focus. By leveraging this precious time strategically, many fledgling businesses have taken flight. Consider Linh, an office worker with a penchant for organic skincare. Recognizing a gap in the market for all-natural products that could be whipped up in a home kitchen, she spent her weekends crafting lotions and potions. She filmed the process, launching a YouTube channel alongside her Shopify store. Orders surged as viewers became customers, intrigued by watching the creation process. Linh now runs a thriving business, far from her former cubicle life.

For some, the weekend hustle isn't merely about extra money but also about fulfilling a deeper purpose. Mark, a former high school teacher, noticed students struggling with traditional learning methods. Capitalizing on his experience, he devoted his weekends to creating an online learning platform with educational games and interactive lessons. By the end of the first 48 hours, he had a working prototype and a clear vision. Angel investors saw the potential in his project, and his platform now assists thousands of students worldwide, boasting impressive subscription rates.

Then there's Julia, who found her niche in customized fitness plans. Frustrated with generic routines, she designed personalized fitness plans that catered to specific needs, from postpartum recovery to athletic performance. Over one weekend, she crafted a stunning website, optimized for user experience, and promoted her service through local gym partnerships and community boards. From those modest beginnings, she scaled rapidly, eventually launching a mobile app that attracts users internationally. Her story underscores the potential to turn personal frustration into lucrative solutions.

What do these stories share in common? Each of these entrepreneurs identified a need, used the limited time of a weekend to take decisive action, and leveraged the power of focused work. They didn't wait for perfect conditions; they seized the moment and adapted along the way. This kind of gritty determination and swift execution can provide a solid foundation for future growth.

Another captivating example is Ben, a freelance graphic designer who merged his passion for art with entrepreneurship. Realizing small businesses needed affordable yet high-quality design services, he created a "Design in a Day" service. Over a single weekend, he set up a basic WordPress site, outlining clear packages and using striking visuals of his past work. His marketing strategy included a countdown timer to create urgency and exclusivity. The concept exploded, and within weeks, his weekends were booked solid with clients. He soon expanded to hire other designers and turned his side offering into a digital agency.

These narratives illustrate that a great idea combined with a well-spent weekend can yield astonishing results. Pam, a social worker by profession but an avid gardener by heart, leveraged her green thumb to create urban gardening kits. Over two days, she packaged seeds, soil, and instructional guides into appealing kits and launched them on Etsy. Her story went viral in local newspapers and blogs, spotlighting the simplicity and joy of gardening. Her online store now sees steady traffic, proving that niche markets can thrive if presented innovatively.

Lastly, consider Alex and Sam, a duo passionate about tech and education. They envisioned an interactive coding bootcamp aimed at kids. Over a 48-hour hackathon-style weekend, they developed a series of gamified coding challenges. The swift feedback loop enabled them to refine the user experience promptly. By Sunday's end, they'd launched a beta version and garnered their first batch of users. As schools and parents caught wind, their user base grew exponentially. They now run a successful company that instills essential tech skills in young minds.

These success stories have one clear takeaway: the constraints of a weekend can actually drive creativity and focus. The power of the weekend lies in initiating momentum and achieving tangible results, proving that one well-spent weekend can catalyze monumental change. Achieving a million-dollar business doesn't always require years of toil; sometimes, all it takes is a leap of faith, a clear plan, and two undistracted days.

Chapter 3: Brainstorming the Right Idea

You're eager to jump into the world of entrepreneurial success, but the first hurdle is finding that perfect idea. Start by examining your passions and skills—what do you enjoy doing, and what are you good at? This isn't just about following your heart; it's about matching your inner drive with market demand. Pay close attention to gaps in the market that you can fill, whether it's an unaddressed need or an innovative twist on an existing solution. Involve family, friends, and potential customers in your brainstorming process to gather diverse perspectives and feedback. Make it iterative; don't settle on the first idea that comes to mind. The goal is to amalgamate creativity with practicality, ensuring your big idea has a solid foundation to stand on when it's time to bring it to life. Once you've identified a potential concept, it's crucial to put it to the test swiftly and efficiently—there's no time to waste when you're aiming to launch a million-dollar business in 48 hours.

Identifying Market Gaps

Now that you're ready to brainstorm the right ideas, the first crucial step is identifying market gaps. This requires a keen observational skill, the ability to spot opportunities where existing businesses fall short or where consumer needs remain unmet. Think of it as a treasure hunt, but instead of gold, you're searching for underserved niches in the market that hold potential for innovation and profitability.

The notion of a market gap is rooted in human behavior and its evolving nature. Consumer preferences, technology advancements, and socio-economic trends necessitate continual adaptation. For instance, consider how food delivery services boomed by identifying the need for convenience among urban dwellers. Likewise, identifying gaps is about questioning the status quo and envisioning how things could be better, faster, or simpler.

This process begins with critical observation. Look at existing products and services and ask fundamental questions: What could be improved? Where are customers experiencing pain points? And perhaps most importantly, what needs are not being met at all? Real-life examples like Airbnb or Uber started by simply recognizing unmet needs in existing industries—hospitality and transportation, respectively—and then creating solutions tailored to those gaps.

As you explore potential gaps, it's essential to couple speculation with solid research. Start by diving into customer reviews of products or services similar to what you have in mind. Online forums, social media groups, and Q&A sites are treasure troves of candid consumer opinions. The frustrations and desires expressed by consumers are direct indicators of where gaps might exist. Pay close attention to recurring themes in complaints and wish lists; these often point to common issues that many people face.

Next, perform a SWOT analysis—assessing the Strengths, Weaknesses, Opportunities, and Threats related to your potential idea. This framework helps you to thoroughly analyze the landscape in which your idea will exist and exposes areas that demand improvement or innovation. A common error is to rely solely on intuition without supporting evidence. Therefore, balance your gut feelings with data-driven insights to create a more robust idea.

Don't shy away from the competition; embrace it. Scrutinizing your competitors can offer valuable lessons. There's a powerful saying: "Good artists borrow; great artists steal." This doesn't mean literally copying ideas but learning from competitors' successes and failures to find your unique twist. Recognize what competitors are doing well and identify where they falter. Sometimes, it's not about reinventing the wheel but improving its design for better efficiency and user experience.

Seasonality and trends also play a significant role. While trend-based businesses can be lucrative, they come with higher risk. Keep an eye on emerging trends, but also consider how sustained consumer behavior is evolving. A blend of capitalizing on today's trends and preparing for future shifts can position you ahead of the curve. Remember, the ultimate goal is to anticipate market needs before your competitors do.

A useful exercise is to engage in ethnographic research, which involves observing people in their natural environments. This can uncover unarticulated needs that traditional market research might miss. By immersing yourself in the customer experience, you gain firsthand insight into challenges and inefficiencies that your business could address. Visiting marketplaces, attending trade shows, and casually talking to potential customers can reveal a wealth of information.

If you're looking to harness technology, consider how emerging technological advancements can be applied innovatively to fill market gaps. Often, the intersection of new tech and traditional industries yields groundbreaking ideas. For instance, the development of augmented reality (AR) has found applications in retail, gaming, and even real estate, significantly disrupting these markets. Always be on the lookout for technological innovations that can usher in unprecedented solutions to perennial problems.

Remember, iterating on existing solutions with a unique value proposition can effectively fill a market gap. For instance, if you notice that people love gourmet coffee but find it expensive and inconvenient, your solution could be a subscription box offering high-quality, ready-to-brew coffee delivered to their doorsteps. It's about improving accessibility, affordability, and convenience while maintaining high quality.

Connecting with potential customers directly can offer priceless feedback. Engage in conversations, conduct surveys, and participate in community discussions to gauge interest levels and gather opinions. The questions you ask should delve into their preferences, dislikes, and aspirations. The primary objective is to understand the customer deeply, enabling you to personalize your offering to fit their exact needs.

Be mindful of cultural perceptions and economic factors that could influence market gaps. In some regions, what might be considered a gap could already be well-served in another area due to varying social dynamics. A thorough understanding of cultural nuances can provide an edge in tailoring your solutions appropriately.

Lastly, keep the bigger picture in sight—solving market gaps isn't just about making a profit; it's also about generating value for your customers. The most successful businesses address critical pain points while adding significant, meaningful value to their users' lives. By adopting this mindset, you'll be more inspired to seek out worthwhile gaps that resonate with consumers on a deeper level.

In conclusion, identifying market gaps is an artful blend of curiosity, research, and strategy. It involves questioning existing norms, delving into consumer pain points, and capitalizing on new opportunities that others might overlook. By aligning your business concept with genuine consumer needs and staying adaptable to market changes, you're on your way to uncovering the next lucrative opportunity.

Validating Your Ideas Quickly

Speed is of the essence when it comes to validating your business ideas quickly. You've brainstormed a promising concept, but how do you know it's worth pursuing? The faster you can test the viability of your idea, the quicker you can pivot or push forward with confidence. This approach allows you to save both time and resources, focusing only on ideas that have the potential to turn into a profitable venture.

The first step in validating your idea is to understand the core problem you're solving. Does your idea address a significant pain point, or are you simply offering a nice-to-have product? To gauge this, conduct a quick preliminary survey among your target audience. Utilize tools like Google Forms or SurveyMonkey to ask a few key questions. Keep it short, around 5-10 questions, focusing on the problem's severity and current gaps in the market. This initial feedback can provide critical insights into the problem's magnitude and your idea's relevance.

One of the most effective ways to validate your idea is through landing pages. Create a simple one-page website that outlines your product or service, emphasizing its benefits and unique selling points. Use a clear call-to-action, such as asking visitors to sign up for updates or early access. Tools like Unbounce, Leadpages, or even a WordPress template can help you set up a landing page quickly. Track metrics such as conversion rates and user engagement to measure interest.

Social media is another powerful tool for validation. Platforms like Instagram, Facebook, and Twitter allow you to reach a broad audience without significant upfront costs. Create a few compelling posts or ads explaining your idea and direct traffic to your landing page. Monitor the response closely. High engagement, shares, and comments are strong indicators that your idea resonates with people. You can also employ A/B testing on these platforms to compare different aspects of your concept, such as pricing or features.

Before diving into full-scale production, consider creating a Minimum Viable Product (MVP). An MVP is a stripped-down version of your product that includes only the essential features necessary to meet the primary needs of your target audience. Releasing an MVP allows you to gather real-world feedback, spot potential issues early, and make informed adjustments. Platforms like Kickstarter and Indiegogo can also serve as springboards, enabling you to gauge market enthusiasm and even secure initial funding.

Having conversations with potential customers is invaluable. Arrange brief interviews or focus groups to dig deeper into their needs, preferences, and pain points. Direct interaction can uncover insights that surveys and landing pages might miss. Ask open-ended questions and listen carefully. The qualitative data gathered can offer a richer understanding of your market's desires and challenges.

Don't overlook the value of competitive analysis in your validation process. Investigate how other businesses are addressing similar problems. Are there glaring weaknesses in their offerings that your idea could exploit? Identify what they're doing right and where they fall short. This analysis not only helps validate your idea but also sharpens your strategic edge. Utilize tools like SEMrush or Ahrefs to dig into competitor metrics and uncover actionable data.

Another rapid validation technique is to offer a pre-sale or reservation system. If people are willing to pay for your product before it even exists, you're onto something significant. Use platforms like Shopify or WooCommerce to set up a quick e-commerce site where visitors can reserve your product. This approach not only validates interest but also provides a financial commitment, solidifying the demand.

Pitch your idea to a community of early adopters. Online forums like Reddit, Quora, and even niche Facebook groups are fertile grounds for feedback. Present your idea and solicit opinions. These communities are often brutally honest, offering constructive criticism that can help refine your concept. Engage actively in these discussions, show genuine interest in the feedback, and be prepared to pivot if necessary.

In the digital age, data is gold. Utilize analytics to your advantage. Track website traffic, social media metrics, and email open rates meticulously. Tools like Google Analytics, Hotjar, and Crazy Egg can provide detailed insights into user behavior. Understanding how people interact with your content can reveal what resonates and what falls flat, offering clues on how to optimize your idea further.

Remember, validation is an ongoing process. The market evolves, and so should your approach. Continuously gather feedback, analyze data, and be willing to make adjustments. Even after a successful launch, stay vigilant and open to change. The ability to adapt quickly to market feedback can differentiate a thriving business from a stagnant one.

Lastly, let's talk about the psychological aspect of validation. Many entrepreneurs are emotionally attached to their ideas, which can sometimes cloud judgment. It's crucial to remain objective during the validation process. Look at the data with a critical eye and be prepared to make hard decisions. If your idea isn't getting the traction you hoped for, it's better to know early so you can pivot or move on to the next potential success.

In summary, validating your ideas quickly is a multifaceted endeavor requiring a balance of speed, strategic thinking, and open-mindedness. By leveraging tools like surveys, landing pages, social media, MVPs, and direct customer interactions, you can gather essential data rapidly. Trust the process, remain flexible, and keep your eyes on the ultimate goal—transforming your concept into a million-dollar business with minimal wasted effort.

Chapter 4: Research and Preparation

You've got your million-dollar idea, but before diving headfirst into execution, it's crucial to lay the groundwork with thorough research and preparation. Start by knowing your audience inside and out; understanding who they are, what they need, and how your product or service fits into their lives can make or break your venture. Next, dive into analyzing your competition. Identify their strengths and weaknesses, learn from their successes and failures, and discover opportunities they might have missed. This dual approach of customer insight and competitive analysis equips you with the knowledge to craft a strategy that stands out in the crowded marketplace. The time you invest now in research and preparation will pay dividends when it comes to building a business that not only survives but thrives.

Knowing Your Audience

Understanding who you're selling to is perhaps one of the most critical steps in turning your weekend hustle into a million-dollar business. Your audience is not a monolithic entity but a diverse group with varying needs, desires, and pain points. Recognizing these differences and tailoring your product, marketing, and even your brand voice can make the difference between struggle and success. It's not just about having a brilliant idea; it's about having an idea that resonates with the people who will be paying for it.

First, it's essential to paint a clear picture of your target audience. Who are they? What do they do? What problems are they facing that your product or service can solve? One way to start is by creating customer personas. These personas should include demographic information such as age, gender, occupation, and income level, but also delve deeper into psychographic details—interests, hobbies, values, and lifestyle choices. When visualizing who these people are, it becomes easier to tailor your offerings precisely to their needs.

Take, for instance, a side hustler interested in launching an eco-friendly cleaning product. A broad market approach would be too vague and ineffective. Instead, focus on individuals who are environmentally conscious, perhaps young parents looking for safe alternatives to chemical cleaners or millennials who prioritize sustainability. Knowing your audience can inform everything from the product's ingredients to its packaging and marketing language.

The next step involves market research. Utilize online tools and platforms like Google Trends, social media analytics, and survey tools to gather data on your target audience. Are there forums, groups, or online communities where your ideal customers congregate? Engaging directly with these communities can provide invaluable insights. This is critical because data-driven decisions are generally more accurate than assumptions or guesses. Understanding the search habits, social media behaviors, and purchasing trends of your audience will help refine your approach.

Another valuable approach is competitor analysis, which will be discussed in the following section but is worth mentioning here. By examining who your competitors are targeting and how they interact with their audience, you can uncover gaps in the market. What are customers saying in reviews? Are there common complaints or praises? This information provides a rich ground for further understanding your audience and finding ways to differentiate yourself.

It's not enough to identify your audience once and call it a day; this is an ongoing process. As your business grows, so will your audience, and their needs may evolve. Being adaptable and staying updated with continuous market research will ensure you remain relevant. Use tools like Google Analytics to track audience behavior on your website. What pages are they visiting the most? Where are they dropping off? This analytical approach keeps your finger on the pulse, allowing you to pivot when necessary.

Remember, communication with your audience matters immensely. The language you use should resonate with them. Are you targeting young, tech-savvy professionals? Incorporate contemporary slang and a witty tone. If your audience comprises more traditional consumers, perhaps a more formal tone would be appropriate. Your message should reflect an understanding of their unique experiences and perspectives.

Feedback loops are also critical. Your audience's feedback should be the guiding light for improvements and pivots. Set up systems for collecting regular feedback through surveys, social media interactions, or customer service channels. And don't just gather feedback—act on it. This not only enhances customer satisfaction but also fosters a sense of community and loyalty. When people see that their opinions matter, they are more likely to become repeat customers.

Storytelling is an underutilized yet profoundly effective method to connect with your audience. Share stories about why you started your business, challenges you've faced, and milestones you've achieved. Such narratives add a human element to your brand, making it more relatable. People don't just buy products; they buy the stories and values behind those products. So, weave your story into your brand narrative, making it an extension of the audience's aspirations and dreams.

On a practical note, consider segmenting your audience for highly targeted marketing campaigns. Different segments may respond to different messages. For example, an email campaign promoting a 20% discount on your product may appeal to price-sensitive segments, whereas a campaign highlighting your product's premium features might be more effective for value-driven consumers. By delivering the right message to the right audience, you maximize the impact of your marketing efforts.

Lastly, never underestimate the power of personalization. In a world where consumers are bombarded with generic messages, personalized communication can cut through the noise. Use your data to send targeted messages, personalized emails, and customized offers. Personalization makes your audience feel valued, which in turn fosters loyalty. For instance, addressing customers by their first names in emails or recommending products based on their past purchases can significantly boost engagement and conversions.

Your audience is the cornerstone of your business. Thoroughly understanding who they are, what they want, and how they behave will guide your decisions and help you create a product or service that truly meets their needs. Master this, and you're well on your way to turning that weekend idea into a million-dollar venture.

Analyzing the Competition

You've got a business idea that you think could be the next big thing. But hold on—before you dive headfirst into it, you need to take a good, hard look at who else is playing in your sandbox. Analyzing the competition isn't just a box to check off; it's a critical component of succeeding in any business venture. Think of it as the recon mission that gives you insights into what you're up against and where you can shine.

First things first, let's identify your competitors. You can't analyze what you don't see. At a basic level, competitors fall into two categories: direct and indirect. Direct competitors offer the same products or services that you do. If you plan on starting a coffee shop, other coffee shops in your area are your direct competition. Indirect competitors, on the other hand, don't offer the same product but satisfy the same need. In this case, a cafe offering juices could be considered indirect competition. Knowing who your competitors are is the foundational step in strategically positioning yourself in the market.

Once you've identified your competitors, map out their strengths and weaknesses. Don't skip this step—it's invaluable. Visit their websites, social media pages, and physical locations if possible. Check their product lines, customer reviews, and any available financial information. Are they active on social media? Do they engage well with their audience? Do they have a lot of resources? All these questions help you understand where they excel and where they fall short.

Next, you should critically evaluate their pricing strategies. Pricing isn't just about numbers; it's about perception. Is your competitor positioning themselves as a premium brand with higher prices, or do they offer value for money? Your goal is to find gaps. Maybe they're overcharging or providing less value, giving you an opportunity to offer a better deal to attract price-sensitive customers. On the flip side, if they provide a premium product, there might be a niche market willing to pay more for enhanced features or better quality.

Observing marketing strategies of competitors can provide golden insights. Pay attention to their advertising, promotions, and public relations efforts. How are they attracting and retaining customers? Are there specific channels or platforms they are heavily investing in? Understanding these tactics can offer clues about what works and, equally important, what doesn't. This can save you both time and money as you develop your own marketing strategy.

Dig into customer feedback and reviews about your competitors. Sites like Yelp, Google Reviews, and industry-specific forums can give you raw, unfiltered insights into customer experiences. Are customers constantly complaining about one specific issue, like poor customer service or frequent product malfunctions? Such weaknesses can be turned into your strengths. Address these pain points right from the start to win over disgruntled customers looking for better options.

Don't forget to analyze their online presence. In today's digital age, how a company presents itself online is often just as important as its offline presence. Look at their website—how user-friendly is it? Examine their content strategy—are they publishing blogs, videos, or podcasts? How engaging is their social media presence? Analyzing these aspects helps you refine your digital strategy, potentially giving you a competitive edge.

Competitive analysis isn't a one-time task; it's an ongoing process. Markets evolve, new competitors enter, and customer preferences change. Make it a habit to routinely check up on competitors to stay informed of any shifts or trends. Set up Google Alerts for key competitors and industry terms to keep tabs on real-time developments. You don't want to be blindsided by a new entrant or a major strategic pivot from an existing competitor.

Moreover, you can learn a lot from the mistakes and successes of your competitors. Failures shouldn't just be seen as pitfalls but as valuable lessons.

If a major player rolls out a new service and it flops, analyze why. Was it poorly timed, overpriced, or just not in demand? The same goes for their wins. If they launch a successful loyalty program, try to dissect the elements that made it work and consider how you might adapt those to fit your own business model.

It's also useful to understand the influence of macroeconomic factors on your competitors. Economic downturns, technological advancements, and regulatory changes all impact how businesses operate. Analyzing how your competitors respond to these external factors can offer you a blueprint for your own strategies. If a competitor adapts well to economic shifts, it could provide you with a model for resilience in your own business.

Finally, consider collaborating with or learning from your competitors instead of solely focusing on outmaneuvering them. Networking events, industry forums, and even informal meetups can offer opportunities for partnerships or knowledge sharing that might be mutually beneficial. Sometimes, a strategic partnership can provide a competitive advantage that goes beyond what you could achieve alone.

In conclusion, analyzing the competition is your secret weapon for ensuring your business not only survives but thrives. It's about more than just knowing who you're up against; it's about leveraging that knowledge to carve out your own unique space in the market. This is the foundational work that will inform your strategies in marketing, pricing, customer engagement, and much more. And with this insight, you're not just ready to enter the marketplace—you're ready to dominate it.

Chapter 5: Setting Up Shop

So you've done your research and preparation, and now it's time to set up shop. First, you'll need to choose a business model that fits both your lifestyle and goals; whether it's e-commerce, a service-based business, or something entirely unique, make sure it aligns with your vision. Next, craft a robust business plan that acts as your North Star, guiding your every move and keeping you focused on your objectives. Use this opportunity to outline everything from your target market to your marketing strategies. Think of your business plan as the blueprint to your million-dollar idea—it's essential for attracting investors, securing loans, and keeping yourself on track. Remember, every great structure starts with a solid foundation.

Choosing a Business Model

Choosing a business model is a foundational step in setting up your shop that can significantly impact your ability to reach a million-dollar mark quickly. Whether you're a side hustler, a stay-at-home mom, or a young entrepreneur in your twenties, understanding the different types of business models will help you select one that aligns with your skills, resources, and market demand. This will set you on a fast track to revenue generation within a remarkably short span, such as the 48-hour window you're aiming for.

First, let's delve into the core idea of what a business model actually is. At its simplest, a business model is a plan for how a company creates, delivers, and captures value. It's the strategy for turning your business idea into a profitable enterprise. This can range from traditional models like retail stores and service-based businesses to more modern approaches such as subscriptions and digital products. Identifying the right business model helps you outline how you will serve your customers, generate income, and achieve profitability.

One popular business model is the **freemium model**. This approach allows you to offer a basic version of your product or service for free, while charging for premium features. It works well for digital products, apps, and online services where the cost of serving additional free users is minimal. This model not only attracts a large user base quickly but also creates opportunities for upselling.

Another model to consider is **subscription-based services**. This approach involves charging customers a recurring fee to gain access to a service or product. Subscription models are incredibly effective in creating a consistent and predictable revenue stream. Whether it's a box of curated goods delivered monthly or a continuous access to software, this model helps in building a loyal customer base that can multiply over time.

For those who prefer tangible products, the **e-commerce retail model** might be the best fit. Setting up an online store to sell goods directly to consumers allows you to reach a global audience with relatively low overhead. Nowadays, platforms like Shopify, WooCommerce, and Etsy make it incredibly easy to get started over a weekend. You can also explore dropshipping to minimize inventory costs and logistical headaches.

If you're more inclined towards providing services, consider the **service-based business model**. This could range from consulting and freelance services to physical services like home cleaning or landscaping. The key here is to leverage your skills and expertise to offer solutions to problems that individuals or businesses are facing. The service model often has higher margins, but it might also require more of your time and personal involvement initially.

One unique business model gaining traction is the **marketplace model**. This involves creating a platform where buyers and sellers can interact. Examples include Amazon for general goods, Etsy for handmade products, or even services like Airbnb. The marketplace model capitalizes on network effects: as you get more buyers and sellers, the platform becomes more valuable.

While more complex to establish, the scalability of this model can lead to exponential growth.

It's also worth exploring **affiliate marketing** if you're keen on building an audience first and selling later. In this model, you promote other businesses' products and earn a commission for every sale made through your referral. This is particularly effective for bloggers, influencers, and social media enthusiasts who can generate income without maintaining inventory or dealing with customer service.

Moreover, with the rise of technology, the **software as a service (SaaS) model** has become increasingly popular. By offering software solutions via subscription, businesses can earn consistent revenue while providing continuous updates and improvements to their customers. The initial development might be resource-intensive, but the potential for scalability is tremendous.

Another innovative model is the **peer-to-peer (P2P) model**, where users interact directly to buy, sell, or rent goods and services. Think about platforms like eBay for selling items or Uber and Lyft for ride-sharing services. This model can foster community while leveraging the assets and skills of individuals without the need for significant upfront investment.

When choosing a business model, it's crucial to consider your target audience and the value you're providing them. Ask yourself questions like: Who are my customers? What problems am I solving for them? How much are they willing to pay for the solution I offer? Understanding your audience will help you tailor your business model to meet their needs and expectations.

Another critical aspect is evaluating your competition. What business models are your competitors using? How successful are they, and what can you learn from them? This research will give you insights into what works and what doesn't in your specific market, allowing you to refine your approach.

To sum up, selecting a business model is no trivial task, but it doesn't have to be daunting either. Consider your strengths, market needs, and the speed at which you intend to scale. The right business model will not only help you get started efficiently but will also set the stage for rapid growth and long-term success. Remember, the aim is to create, deliver, and capture value in a way that aligns with your goals and resources. Choose wisely, and the rest of your entrepreneurial journey will be that much smoother.

Creating a Business Plan

Creating a solid business plan isn't just a box to tick off; it's the backbone of your new venture and the roadmap to your million-dollar idea. You've already brainstormed that killer idea and validated its potential; now it's time to put everything on paper. Not only does a business plan help you stay focused, but it's also crucial if you ever need to attract investors or secure funding. Here's how you can build a robust business plan within the confines of a weekend.

The first critical element is the **Executive Summary**. Think of this as a concise elevator pitch for your business. Even though it's the first section of the business plan, it's usually the last one you write. Give an overview of what your business is all about, the problem it solves, and your unique selling proposition. This should be compelling enough to catch the attention of potential investors or partners.

Next up is the **Business Description and Vision**. This part provides more detail about the nature of your business and the market needs you are addressing. You want to include your mission statement here—why does your business exist? What are its goals? Define the long-term vision for your business. Is it scalable? Where do you see it in five, ten years? This section requires you to think beyond the immediate hustle of setting up shop and actually visualize the future.

The **Market Analysis** follows, and this is your chance to showcase your research. Detail your target market, its size, and the demographics of your potential customers. Explain what market need your product or service will fulfill. Include a competitive analysis: who are your main competitors? What are they doing well, and where are they failing? By understanding the competitive landscape, you'll know where you can excel and differentiate yourself.

Now, onto your **Organization and Management Structure**. Who's in charge and what are their roles? Layout your business's legal structure—

whether it's a sole proprietorship, LLC, or corporation. Highlight the key members of your team, their backgrounds, and the roles they will play. Even if you're a solo entrepreneur, you will at some point need to outsource or partner with others. Detail any future positions you foresee as essential for growth.

In the **Products or Services Line**, delve into what you're selling. Describe your products or services in detail. What makes them unique? How do they solve problems? Include information on any research and development you've done, and outline future products or services you plan to introduce. The goal here is to demonstrate that you have a clear vision for the evolution of your offerings.

The next section is crucial: **Marketing and Sales Strategies**. You've got a great product or service, but how will you get it into the hands of customers? Describe your marketing strategy in detail. Are you leveraging social media, email marketing, or other channels? Define your sales strategy and thought process behind pricing. What does the customer journey look like from awareness to purchase?

Don't forget the **Financial Projections**. Even if you're just starting out, put some thought into your financial plan. Detail your revenue models, projected profits, and any expected expenses. Break these figures down by month for the first year, then quarterly for the next few years. This will give you—and any potential backers—a clear picture of your business's financial viability. If you have data from similar ventures, use it to justify your estimates.

The **Funding Request** is relevant if you need external financing. Specify how much capital you need and how you will use it. Be precise. Whether you plan to spend on marketing, equipment, or inventory, outline your financial needs and how they will contribute to your startup's growth. This level of detail shows potential investors that you've done your homework and are serious about your venture.

Finally, tie it all together with an **Appendix**. This section can hold any supplementary information that's too bulky to fit into the main sections but still critical. Include resumes, permits, lease agreements, legal documentation, or product images. An appendix ensures that your business plan remains concise and focused while still providing important details.

Creating a business plan is more than just an exercise; it's an invaluable tool that provides a structured approach to your entrepreneurial journey. It helps clarify your vision, strategize your approach, and set you up for immediate and future success. Take the time to craft a thorough business plan this weekend; you'll thank yourself later when you hit those million-dollar milestones.

Chapter 6: Funding Your Business

Whether you're launching a tech startup from your garage or a boutique bakery from your kitchen, securing the funds to get started can be the linchpin to your success. As an aspiring entrepreneur, consider bootstrapping first, leveraging your savings, personal assets, or even revenue from initial sales to fuel your growth. This approach enables you to maintain control and avoid debt. However, if your vision requires more significant capital, alternative financing options like crowdfunding, angel investors, or small business loans can bridge the gap. Each route has its own set of pros and cons, so think strategically about what aligns best with your business goals and risk tolerance. The key is to make smart, informed decisions that position you for both short-term victories and long-term achievements.

Bootstrapping Basics

Bootstrapping is the art of starting and growing your business from the bottom up with minimal external investment. It's about leveraging your existing resources, maximizing efficiency, and prioritizing frugality to get your idea off the ground. For new entrepreneurs, particularly those looking to build a million-dollar business in a mere 48 hours, understanding the principles of bootstrapping is crucial. It lays the foundation for a robust business that's not reliant on external funding right out of the gate.

So, what does bootstrapping really look like? Imagine you're starting a bakery. Instead of renting a swanky storefront, you begin by selling baked goods out of your home kitchen. Instead of splurging on a professional-grade oven, you make do with what you have, improving as you go. This approach may seem humble, but it's strategic. By keeping your initial costs low, you reduce your risk and give yourself the flexibility to pivot as needed without a financial noose around your neck.

One of the core tenets of bootstrapping is reinvesting profits back into the business. Every dollar made is a dollar that should be considered for growth. Initially, this might mean long hours and personal sacrifices, but the payoff can be significant. For instance, web developers often start small by taking on freelance projects. The income generated is then cycled back into their own software ventures, allowing them to scale progressively without outside help.

Prioritizing essential expenditures is another key component. It's tempting to spend on bells and whistles, but figuring out what's truly necessary for your business's survival and growth is critical. Utilize basic, cost-effective tools and services. You don't need the most advanced software when starting out, just something that gets the job done. Over time, as your business grows, you can then afford to invest in more sophisticated resources.

Another strategy involves leveraging your existing skills and networks. Many successful entrepreneurs start by monetizing what they already know or have passion for. If you're a graphic designer, for example, you can begin by offering design services. This not only brings in initial revenue but also hones your craft, expands your portfolio, and builds your reputation—all at minimal cost.

Beyond your own skills, look to your network for support. Friends, family, and professional connections can offer not just moral support but potential resources as well. This could be in the form of mentorship, free or discounted services, or even word-of-mouth marketing. When you're bootstrapping, leaning on your community isn't just helpful; it's often essential.

Bootstrapping also forces you to validate your business idea quickly. Without deep pockets to fall back on, you need to ensure there is a demand for your product or service right from the start. This could mean launching a minimally viable product (MVP) or leveraging pre-sales to gauge interest and secure some initial funds. Crowdfunding platforms are particularly useful here, allowing you to test the waters and gather customer feedback before making larger investments.

Frugality in bootstrapping is not just about spending little but spending wisely. For instance, instead of a pricey marketing campaign, utilize grassroots marketing efforts. Social media, blog posts, and community events can all serve as platforms to get your message out without breaking the bank. A well-maintained social media presence or a compelling blog can draw unexpected organic traffic and customer interest at no cost.

Time management is another critical aspect. When you're bootstrapping, you're likely juggling multiple roles. Each minute becomes incredibly valuable, and mastering time management can be the difference between success and failure. Break down your tasks into manageable chunks, prioritize what's most important, and be relentless in optimizing your schedule. Tools like Trello or Asana are perfect for keeping track of various responsibilities without any initial upfront costs.

Crucial, yet often overlooked, is the mindset of a bootstrapper. It's a blend of optimism and meticulous calculation. One must balance the visionary attitude required to identify and seize opportunities with the realistic approach of managing limited resources. Keeping a clear, focused vision of your goals will help steer you through the hard times while celebrating small victories along the journey will maintain the morale.

Don't underestimate the power of storytelling when bootstrapping your business. A compelling narrative can attract customers, partners, and even investors down the line. Share your journey, your struggles, and your triumphs. Authenticity resonates with people, and building an emotional connection can drive loyalty and support that monetary investment alone might not achieve.

Despite the challenges, remember that many iconic companies started with bootstrapping. Apple began in a garage, while Facebook was created in a dorm room. Their founders utilized whatever resources they had and focused on creating value first. These stories are a reminder that resource constraints can foster creativity and innovation, pushing you to find unique solutions to problems.

That said, bootstrapping isn't without its risks and limitations. It can sometimes be a slow path to growth, and there will be moments when the lack of financial cushion feels like a significant hurdle. But therein lies its beauty: it encourages resourcefulness, resilience, and a deep understanding of your business from the ground up.

Finally, never forget the importance of continual learning. The business world is always evolving, and staying informed about new tools, trends, and techniques can help you adapt and thrive. Whether through online courses, networking events, or simply reading up on industry news, this ongoing education can offer fresh insights and ideas that fuel your bootstrapping journey.

In conclusion, bootstrapping is about more than just finances; it's a foundational mindset for building a sustainable and resilient business. By leveraging personal resources, maintaining strategic frugality, and focusing on building real value, you set the stage for organic growth. This approach not only minimizes initial risk but also lays the groundwork for a business that stands on its own feet, ready to scale when the time is right.

Alternative Financing Options

When it comes to starting a business quickly, securing funding can seem like a major hurdle. But don't let that slow you down. Traditional bank loans aren't the only game in town; there are many other avenues you can explore to get the capital you need to launch your million-dollar idea. Depending on your business model and the amount of funding required, alternative financing options can offer the flexibility and speed you need to get your business off the ground. Let's dive into some of the most promising alternatives and see how they might align with your goals.

If you don't want to go the usual loan route, one of the first options to consider is crowdfunding. Platforms like Kickstarter and Indiegogo have helped countless entrepreneurs turn their visions into reality. It's not just about the money; crowdfunding can also offer valuable market validation. When potential customers are willing to back your project before it's even launched, you know you're onto something solid. The key to a successful crowdfunding campaign is a compelling story and a well-thought-out rewards system that entices people to back your project.

Another increasingly popular option is peer-to-peer lending. Websites such as LendingClub and Prosper connect borrowers directly with individual investors, cutting out the banking middleman. This can often result in lower interest rates and more flexible terms. One thing to keep in mind is that these platforms look at your creditworthiness, so having a decent credit score can greatly help your case. Nevertheless, the streamlined application process and relatively quick fundraising period make peer-to-peer lending worth considering.

For those who already have some savings but not quite enough to cover the entire start-up cost, microfinancing can be a lifeline. Organizations like Kiva offer small loans, often with lower interest rates and more lenient approval processes. Microloans can be especially helpful for businesses needing less capital to start up but still requiring a financial boost. These loans are typically offered by non-profits that are more interested in seeing your business succeed than making a profit.

Angel investors are another path to consider, especially for more substantial funding needs. These affluent individuals are willing to invest in startups in exchange for equity. What sets angel investors apart is their willingness to take on higher risks for potentially high rewards. Finding the right angel investor involves networking, creating a solid pitch, and demonstrating that you have a sound business plan. The good news? Many angels provide not just funds but also valuable mentorship and connections that can help your business grow.

Don't underestimate the power of business incubators and accelerators. These programs offer much more than just funding; they provide mentorship, networking opportunities, and sometimes even office space. Notable programs like Y Combinator and Techstars have helped launch numerous successful startups. While getting into these programs can be highly competitive, the benefits are tremendous, making them well worth considering.

If you're looking for flexibility, consider revenue-based financing. Unlike traditional loans that involve fixed payments, this option allows you to repay based on your monthly revenue. The repayment amount fluctuates with your business's performance, which can relieve some pressure during slower months. Companies like Lighter Capital offer revenue-based financing tailored to tech startups but can certainly be applicable to other sectors.

Another unconventional yet effective route could be entering competitions and applying for grants. Business plan competitions often come with monetary rewards that can give you the initial funding boost needed. Look for local or industry-specific competitions and grant opportunities. Some cities and states offer grants to promote small businesses, and organizations like the Small Business Innovation Research program provide grants for businesses that contribute to technological innovation.

Believe it or not, your credit card might also be an alternative financing option, albeit with risks. Personal and business credit cards offer a fast way to secure funds and can be convenient for smaller purchases and operational costs. However, the high interest rates can quickly add up, making this a viable option only if you have a solid repayment plan. Used wisely, credit cards can bridge the gap between needing capital and securing more stable funding.

For entrepreneurs eyeing specialized equipment or inventory, vendor financing might be the way to go. Some suppliers allow you to buy now and pay later, often with favorable interest rates or without interest if you meet specific requirements. This could free up your cash flow for other critical expenses in the early stages of your business.

Convertible notes are another innovative financing option, blending features of equity and debt. This instrument allows investors to loan money to your startup, with the idea that the loan will convert into equity at a later date, usually during your next financing round. Convertible notes can speed up the fundraising process and delay the need to value your company until it has grown more.

A less explored but still viable option is using retirement funds to start your business. Self-Directed IRAs or Rollover for Business Startups (ROBS) allow you to invest retirement money into your startup without early withdrawal penalties. This option requires careful consideration and professional guidance to ensure compliance with IRS regulations.

In today's digital age, cryptocurrency and blockchain technology also offer alternative paths for raising capital. Initial Coin Offerings (ICOs) and Security Token Offerings (STOs) let businesses raise funds by issuing digital tokens. While this space is still highly speculative and regulated differently across jurisdictions, it represents a cutting-edge option for tech-savvy entrepreneurs.

Family and friends can also be a valuable resource. While mixing business with personal relationships can be tricky, it's possible to draw up clear agreements to protect both parties. Informal loans or equity investments from those who believe in you can provide the initial push needed to succeed. Just remember to treat these arrangements with the same professionalism as any other business transaction to avoid misunderstandings.

Finally, don't overlook the potential of pre-sales. If your business model allows it, selling products or services before they are fully operational can generate the capital required to complete development. This approach not only funds your business but also validates market demand, increasing your chances of long-term success.

As you can see, there are plenty of alternative financing options available, each with its advantages and caveats. The key is to evaluate which options align best with your business idea, financial needs, and risk tolerance. With a strategic approach, you can secure the funding required to turn your entrepreneurial dreams into reality, thereby setting the stage for rapid growth and enduring success. Remember, the goal isn't just to get money but to find the right partner or platform that believes in your vision and is willing to support it. Happy fundraising!

Chapter 7: Legal and Administrative Set-Up

Navigating the legal and administrative set-up can seem daunting, but it's a crucial step in transforming your weekend side hustle into a million-dollar business. Before you dive into marketing or product development, you need to establish your business structure and register it with the necessary authorities. Decide whether you're going for an LLC, a sole proprietorship, or another structure that suits your needs. Don't overlook essential legal considerations like obtaining the right permits and licenses, setting up a business bank account, and ensuring you're compliant with local, state, and federal regulations. These initial steps might feel tedious, but they're foundational to protect your business and enable smooth operations. Properly setting up your legal and administrative framework now will save you headaches—and potentially a lot of money—down the line. Remember, every major entrepreneur started at this stage, and so can you. Get this right, and you're laying the groundwork for long-term success and peace of mind.

Business Structure and Registration

When you're about to embark on the thrilling journey of launching a million-dollar business in just 48 hours, the importance of choosing the right business structure and getting appropriately registered can't be overstated. This could be the difference between smooth sailing and a choppy ride filled with legal headaches and administrative hitches. The right business structure serves as the foundation upon which everything else is built, offering benefits tailored to your specific needs.

First, let's talk about the most common types of business structures: sole proprietorships, partnerships, limited liability companies (LLCs), and corporations. Each has its pros and cons, depending on your goals, the nature of your business, and future growth plans. And yes, it's worth taking the time to get this step right because the structure you choose will have long-term implications for your taxes, liability, and even your ability to raise funds.

Let's start with sole proprietorships. If you're planning a small side hustle or a business where you'll be the solo player, this could be a quick and easy option. You'll enjoy complete control, but keep in mind that there's no distinction between you and the business. That means you're personally liable for any debts or legal actions. However, for many, the simplicity is well worth the trade-offs, especially for ventures that don't come with a lot of risks.

If you're not going it alone, a partnership might be a better fit. Partnerships allow two or more people to share the workload, risks, and profits. They can be relatively easy to establish, but a crucial aspect is having a solid partnership agreement in place. This will outline roles, responsibilities, and profit-sharing arrangements, ensuring that all partners are on the same page. The downside? Similar to sole proprietorships, partners can be personally liable for the business's obligations.

Moving on to limited liability companies (LLCs), these structures offer a blend of benefits. They provide the liability protection of a corporation while maintaining the operational flexibility and tax efficiencies of a partnership. For many entrepreneurs, LLCs strike the perfect balance — you won't be personally liable for the business's debts, and you can choose whether to be taxed as a sole proprietor, partnership, or corporation. Additionally, LLCs are relatively straightforward to form and require less paperwork than corporations.

If you have grand ambitions and plan to seek outside investors, a corporation might be the way to go. Corporations offer limited liability protection and can raise capital more easily through the sale of stock. However, they come with more regulatory requirements, double taxation on profits, and a greater burden of paperwork. If you're eyeing substantial growth and possibly taking your company public one day, the extra effort might be well worth it.

After deciding on a business structure, the next crucial step is registration. This process can vary depending on your location, but generally, you'll need to register your business name and secure any necessary permits or licenses. Let's break it down a bit.

First, you'll choose a unique business name and check if it's available. Conduct a search through local and federal databases to ensure it's not already taken. Once your name is verified, you'll need to file it with the appropriate government authorities. For sole proprietorships, this could be as simple as registering a "Doing Business As" (DBA) name. LLCs and corporations usually require more formal registration with the state.

Next, you'll likely need an Employer Identification Number (EIN) from the Internal Revenue Service (IRS). Think of your EIN as a social security number for your business. It's essential for tax purposes and will be required when opening a business bank account or hiring employees. The good news? Applying for an EIN is free and can be done online in just a few minutes.

If your business involves selling physical goods, you might also need to obtain a sales tax permit from your state's tax authority. This allows you to collect sales tax from customers and remit it to the state. Depending on your business activities, additional licenses or permits might be necessary. For instance, businesses in the food industry often need health department permits, while those offering professional services like consulting or accounting might need professional licenses.

For digital entrepreneurs, an eCommerce business might require different types of permits and registrations compared to a brick-and-mortar store. You'll need to ensure your business complies with online sales regulations, which could include digital tax collection or specific industry regulations about data protection and privacy.

Furthermore, consider also whether your business should be trademarked. Your brand name and logo, once established, are valuable things. Registering a trademark can protect your intellectual property from being used without your permission. While this step is optional at the beginning, it can be a wise move to safeguard your brand as you scale.

In addition to state and federal registrations, don't overlook local regulations. Many municipalities require businesses to register locally and obtain a business license. This usually involves a simple application and a nominal fee, but the specifics can vary from place to place.

Also, don't forget to open a business bank account once you're registered. This is a crucial step to ensure your personal and business finances remain separate, which simplifies accounting and protects your personal assets. To open a business account, you'll typically need your EIN, business formation documents, ownership agreements, and possibly your business license, depending on the bank's requirements.

Lastly, stay organized and diligent with compliance. Keep copies of all your registration documents, licenses, and permits. Regularly review and renew them as necessary. Regulatory requirements evolve, and maintaining compliance will save you headaches down the road.

With the right business structure and proper registration, you've laid a solid foundation for your entrepreneurial venture. Once these essential steps are in place, you can shift your focus to building and growing your business with confidence and peace of mind. The path to a million-dollar business may be filled with decisions, but choosing the right structure and registering properly will keep you steady on course. Now, let's get to it and build something amazing!

Essential Legal Considerations

When you're overcoming fear and leaping into your new business venture, it's critical to establish a strong legal foundation. Ignoring essential legal considerations can lead to headaches, and worse yet, expose you to unnecessary risks that could derail your ambitious plans. The first step is choosing the appropriate legal structure for your business—be it a sole proprietorship, partnership, LLC, or corporation. Each structure has its own set of pros and cons, particularly around liability, taxation, and administrative complexity.

Understanding Liability and Risk

Liability protection should top your list of priorities. In a sole proprietorship, for example, your personal assets are not protected; creditors can go after your home or savings if the business fails. In contrast, an LLC or corporation offers a buffer—your personal assets stay safeguarded. This isn't just a minor detail; it's a fundamental shield for your peace of mind. Consider your risk tolerance and personal situation when deciding on your business structure.

Intellectual Property: Guarding Your Ideas

You've brainstormed the right idea, validated it quickly, and you're making progress. Now imagine someone swooping in and stealing your concept or branding. That's a nightmare scenario you want to avoid. Take intellectual property (IP) seriously from the get-go. Trademarks, copyrights, and patents are your key tools for protecting your business ideas, unique products, and brand identity. Filing for a trademark ensures no one else can legally use your business name or logo. Similarly, a patent can protect a unique invention, while copyrights can safeguard unique content, such as your business's written or artistic works.

Contracts and Agreements

Business relationships revolve around trust, but even the best relationships must be cemented in clear, binding contracts. Whether it's a partnership agreement, a vendor contract, or a client service agreement, a well-drafted contract spells out the specifics, leaving no room for misunderstandings. You might think you don't need formal agreements this early, but consider them essential components of your administrative set-up. Remember that verbal agreements don't have the same enforceability as written ones.

Data Privacy: Safeguarding Consumer Information

Data is the new oil, and protecting it is paramount. If your venture involves collecting personal information—be it emails, addresses, or payment details—you must comply with data privacy laws. Regulations like the GDPR (General Data Protection Regulation) in the EU and CCPA (California Consumer Privacy Act) in the U.S. have stringent requirements on how you must handle personal data. Not complying can result in hefty fines and damage to your reputation.

Permits and Licenses: The Hidden Necessities

Depending on your business type and location, you might need various permits and licenses. Operating without the necessary permissions can lead to fines, closures, or legal action. From general business licenses to specific industry-related permits, do your homework to ensure you're compliant. This might seem like mundane paperwork, but it's as essential to your business as your marketing strategy or your product development.

Employment Laws: Building a Workforce

If you plan on hiring employees, even freelancers or part-time help, you need to be aware of the myriad of employment laws. These regulations cover wages, working conditions, benefits, and non-discriminatory practices. Proper employee contracts, payroll setups, and insurance are vital elements to consider. Make sure you're familiar with both federal and state-specific labor laws to avoid any legal entanglements that could arise from mismanagement.

Insurance: An Added Layer of Protection

Another critical, though sometimes overlooked, aspect is insurance. Business insurance can cover everything from property damage to liability claims. Consider general liability insurance at the very least. If you're offering professional services, errors and omissions insurance can protect you from claims of negligence or inadequate work. The right insurance policies act as your safety net, providing a financial cushion against unforeseen setbacks.

Tax Compliance: Keeping the IRS at Bay

Taxes can be a complex topic, but there's no escaping them. Your choice of business structure will impact your tax obligations, and failing to comply with tax requirements can result in severe penalties. Make sure to keep accurate records of all transactions, and consider employing an accountant early on. Some tax responsibilities you must address include income tax, sales tax, and payroll tax, depending on your business activities and location.

Avoiding Legal Pitfalls: Being Proactive

The best way to handle legal challenges is to prevent them in the first place. This means staying informed about changes in the legal landscape that could affect your business. Engage with a legal advisor who understands your industry. Proactivity in legal matters offers a competitive advantage and can save you significant distress down the road. Remember, ignorance is not a defense in the eyes of the law.

Government and Industry Regulations

Lastly, be mindful of specific government and industry regulations that might apply to your business. If you're in healthcare, finance, or another heavily regulated industry, the compliance requirements will be more stringent. Ignoring these regulations isn't an option; it's a legal and ethical necessity. By aligning your operations with these requirements from the outset, you lay a robust foundation for long-term success.

Effective risk management and legal vigilance give you the freedom to focus on what you do best—innovating, creating, and growing your business. Ensuring you address these critical legal considerations properly sets you up for stability and durability, providing the structure you need to turn your weekend venture into a million-dollar success story.

With these legal bases covered, you're not just building a business; you're building a legacy that stands on solid ground. The administrative effort might seem tedious, but it's invaluable. It's your ticket to not just surviving, but thriving in the competitive entrepreneurial landscape. Are you ready for that level of commitment? Because that's what transforms dreams into reality, from an idea sparked over a weekend to a flourishing enterprise.

Chapter 8: Building Your Brand

Creating a powerful brand isn't just about a catchy logo or tagline; it's about shaping the story and identity that resonate with your target audience. Whether you're a side hustler, student, or entrepreneur, your brand is the beacon that'll guide customers to your door. Start by understanding the core values and vision that drive your enterprise, then translate that into every visual and textual element you produce. This isn't just fluff; a solid brand makes you memorable and trusted, driving loyalty and setting you apart from the competition. Remember, your brand is the personality of your business—make it genuine, relatable, and unmistakably yours.

Crafting Your Brand Identity

If you've made it this far, you're already well on your way to being a successful entrepreneur. But a business without a strong identity is like a ship without a compass; it might float but it won't go anywhere intentional. Crafting your brand identity is the cornerstone of "Building Your Brand," and it sets the stage for all the other elements that follow.

So, what exactly is brand identity? Think of it as the personality of your business. It's how you present yourself to the world and how the world perceives you. Your brand identity encompasses everything from your company name, logo, and tagline, to your color palette, typeface, and overall aesthetic. But it's more than just visuals; it's the tone of your communications, the values you stand for, and the experience you promise to deliver to your

CHAPTER 8: BUILDING YOUR BRAND

customers.

The first step in crafting your brand identity is introspection. You need to dig deep and answer some fundamental questions. What is the core mission of your business? What are your values? What differentiates you from your competitors? This isn't just about what you sell; it's about why you exist. For example, are you committed to sustainability, or do you pride yourself on offering unparalleled customer service?

Your answers to these questions will form the backbone of your brand's story. And people don't just buy products; they buy stories and experiences. Take the time to articulate your vision and mission clearly. Write them down and make sure they resonate with both your aspirations and the needs of your target audience.

Once you've nailed down your mission and values, the next step is to decide on your brand's voice and tone. This part might seem abstract, but it's incredibly powerful. Are you fun and quirky, or are you professional and authoritative? Your voice should reflect your brand's personality and should be consistent across all channels—be it your website, social media posts, or customer service emails.

Consistency is key to building a strong brand identity. A disjointed message can confuse your audience and dilute your impact. Imagine a premium coffee brand that uses formal, luxurious language in its product descriptions but suddenly goes casual and slang-heavy on social media. It just doesn't gel, right? Make sure that your tone and voice align with your brand's overall ethos and appeal to your target market.

If you're not a designer by trade, hiring a professional to help you craft the visual aspects of your brand can be a game-changer. A skilled graphic designer can bring your vision to life through an evocative logo, a cohesive color palette, and versatile typography. Your logo is often the first thing people will associate with your business, so it needs to be memorable and reflective of your brand's essence.

Colors, too, play a crucial role in brand identity. Different colors evoke different emotions and perceptions. Blue often signifies trust and professionalism, whereas red can evoke excitement and urgency. Choose colors that align well with the emotions you aim to evoke in your audience. And remember, less is more. A simple, clean palette is usually more impactful than a cluttered and overwhelming mix.

Typography is another subtle yet powerful tool. The fonts you choose should complement your brand's personality and be legible across all media. Think of typography as the voice of your text; it should communicate the same message your words are conveying, only silently.

Your tagline, though not always necessary, can effectively distill your brand's mission and value proposition into a quick, catchy phrase. It's your elevator pitch in under ten words. Whether it's Nike's "Just Do It" or Apple's "Think Different," a strong tagline can become an integral part of your brand's identity.

Now, the visual and communicative aspects are crucial, but what truly cements your brand identity in the hearts and minds of customers is the experience you provide. Your brand identity must be evident in every touchpoint your customers have with your business. From your website user experience to your packaging, customer service, and even your return policy—each interaction should reinforce your brand's values and promise.

For example, if you brand yourself as a luxury brand, every touchpoint should exude quality and exclusivity. Your website should be slick and high-end, your customer service should be impeccable, and your product packaging should feel premium. On the contrary, a brand built on affordability and value should focus on user-friendly design, accessible customer support, and straightforward, no-frills packaging.

As you grow and evolve, your brand identity will naturally need to adapt as well. However, any changes should be thoughtful and strategic, ensuring they align with your core values and mission. Rebranding is not just about changing your logo or website layout; it's about reshaping how you're perceived without losing your essence.

Now, let's talk about the brand promise. This is the commitment you make to your customers. It's what they can expect every time they interact with your brand. Your promise should be clear, compelling, and consistently delivered. For example, a brand like FedEx promises reliable, timely deliveries, and they've built a reputation on fulfilling that promise.

Measuring the success of your brand identity is another crucial element. Use surveys, social media feedback, and customer reviews to gauge how well your brand is resonating with your audience. Pay attention to both the qualitative feedback—like reviews and comments—and quantitative metrics—such as website analytics and sales data. Understanding where you stand can help you fine-tune your identity and messaging for even greater impact.

Lastly, remember that your brand identity is something you need to nurture. Brands are not static; they live and breathe along with market trends and consumer behavior. Keep an eye on industry trends and be willing to innovate and adapt when necessary, but always stay true to your fundamental values and mission.

In conclusion, crafting your brand identity isn't just a task to check off your list; it's the foundation upon which your entire business will stand. It encapsulates who you are, what you stand for, and why customers should choose you over others. Get it right, and you're setting yourself up for a strong, enduring presence in the market that can turn your side hustle into a million-dollar business within 48 hours.

Taking the time to craft a compelling, consistent brand identity will not only attract customers but also turn them into loyal brand advocates. And in the world of business, there's nothing more valuable than that.

Designing a Logo and Tagline

Your logo and tagline are critical elements in building your brand identity, especially when you aim to kickstart a million-dollar business within 48 hours. These two components are often the first interaction potential customers will have with your business. Thus, they must encapsulate your brand's essence in a memorable visual and verbal bite. The power of an effective logo and tagline can't be overstated; they are the face and voice of your brand.

Creating a logo involves more than just combining graphics and text. It should reflect your brand's personality, values, and mission. Think of the most memorable logos you know - Nike, Apple, or McDonald's. Each is a simple yet powerful representation of the company's core essence. Achieving this in less than 48 hours may seem daunting, but with focused effort and clear vision, it's entirely possible.

Your first step is to understand what your brand stands for. Is it innovative, trustworthy, fun, or luxurious? Write down keywords that define your brand and use these as a foundation for your logo's design. If you're bootstrapping and on a tight budget, free tools like Canva or online logo makers can be beneficial. These platforms offer intuitive interfaces and countless templates, allowing even non-designers to produce impressive results.

However, while DIY tools are excellent for getting started, don't shy away from investing in professional help if it fits within your budget. Graphic designers bring a wealth of experience and creativity to the table, often surpassing what can be achieved with templates. Websites like Fiverr or Upwork can connect you with freelance designers who offer competitive rates.

When sketching your logo (even if it's just on a piece of paper), keep these design principles in mind: simplicity, scalability, relevance, and versatility. A successful logo is simple and easily recognizable, whether it's on a billboard or a business card. Scalability ensures that it looks good in various sizes. Relevance means it resonates with your target audience, and versatility ensures it works across different mediums and contexts.

Color psychology plays a significant role in brand perception. Different colors evoke different emotions and responses. For instance, blue often conveys trust and professionalism, making it popular in the tech and finance sectors. On the other hand, green symbolizes health and wellness, widely used in the organic and eco-friendly industries. Choose colors that align with your brand values and the message you want to convey.

Typography is another crucial factor. The font style you choose should complement your logo and brand personality. For example, serif fonts like Times New Roman exude tradition and reliability, whereas sans-serif fonts like Helvetica are modern and clean. Combining fonts can add visual interest but do so sparingly to maintain readability and coherence.

Next, let's shift our focus to the tagline. A well-crafted tagline underscores your logo by succinctly conveying your brand's promise or unique value proposition in a way that's both memorable and evocative. It serves as a mental trigger, helping customers recall your brand and its unique offerings.

Your tagline should be short – ideally, under seven words. Think of Nike's "Just Do It" or Apple's "Think Different." These taglines are memorable, motivational, and closely aligned with the brands' identities. Brainstorm phrases that encapsulate your brand's mission and consider wordplay or rhymes to make it catchy.

Your tagline needs to address the 'why' behind your business. Why does your brand exist? What problem does it solve? How is it different from competitors? Answering these questions will guide you to a strong, impactful tagline.

Once you've crafted a list of potential taglines, test them out. Share them with friends, family, or even your social media followers. Gathering feedback will help you gauge which tagline resonates most with your audience. Crowdsourcing opinions can also provide new perspectives and ideas that you might have overlooked.

In the rapidly moving phase of building a million-dollar business over a weekend, speed and efficiency are your allies. Dedicate a set amount of time for brainstorming, designing, and refining your logo and tagline. Use iterative feedback loops to make quick improvements but avoid getting stuck in the cycle of perfectionism. Remember, it's about creating a strong foundation that you can build upon and refine over time.

Finally, once you have your logo and tagline, use them consistently. Integrate them across all your marketing channels, business cards, website, social media profiles, and product packaging. Consistency builds trust and helps establish your brand's presence in the market swiftly.

To wrap up, designing a logo and tagline might seem like small steps, but they are monumental in your journey of building a recognizable and compelling brand. Make these steps count by focusing on clarity, alignment with brand values, and consistent application. By doing so, you'll not only create a unique brand identity but also set the stage for swift and lasting market recognition.

Chapter 9: Creating a Website

Ready to make your business idea accessible to the world? Creating a website is your gateway to showcasing your product or service and capturing the interest of potential customers. First, choose a domain name that resonates with your brand and is easy to remember. Once you've nailed down a domain, it's time to build your site. You don't need to be a tech wizard—there are plenty of user-friendly platforms like WordPress, Wix, and Squarespace that offer customizable templates. Focus on keeping the design clean, intuitive, and mobile-friendly. Include essential sections like an 'About' page to share your story, a 'Products' or 'Services' page to highlight what you offer, and a 'Contact' page for inquiries. Before you hit "publish," make sure to test your site across different devices and browsers to ensure everything works seamlessly. Launching your site isn't the finish line but the starting point for iterations and improvements based on user feedback. Let's get your digital storefront up and running—you're just a few clicks away from going live!

Choosing a Domain Name

Choosing a domain name might seem like one of those small details you can deal with later, but it's far from trivial. Your domain name is the digital address where your business lives. It needs to be memorable, easy to spell, and capable of establishing credibility with your audience right away. It isn't an exaggeration to say your domain name can make or break your online presence.

First things first, let's talk about the mechanics of a good domain name. Simplicity and clarity are crucial. Your domain name should be easy to remember and type. Think of some of the world's most successful websites—names like Google, Amazon, or Facebook. They're short, catchy, and easy to spell. Ideally, aim for a name that's no more than 12 characters. It might be tempting to add more descriptive words, but it's best to keep it succinct to ensure people can recall it without having to jot it down.

Another key factor is relevance. Your domain name should give people a good idea of what your website is about. If you're running a blog about healthy eating, for instance, including words like "eat," "meal," or "food" can make your domain more intuitive. This helps potential visitors understand your niche at a glance. The goal is to create a connection between your brand and what you offer.

Don't underestimate the power of keywords. Incorporating relevant keywords into your domain name can boost your search engine ranking and make your site more discoverable. However, avoid overstuffing your domain with keywords—this can come off as spammy and tarnish your brand image. For instance, "BestHealthyRecipesForYou.com" is not only cumbersome but also reeks of desperation. A better alternative would be something like "HealthyEats.com."

It's also essential to consider your domain extension, or Top Level Domain (TLD). While .com is the most recognized and trusted TLD, it's not your only option. Extensions like .net, .org, and even newer ones like .io or .co can also work, especially if your ideal .com domain is unavailable. Just remember that .com still holds a certain level of trust and authority in most people's minds.

After selecting a few potential domain names, it's time to check their availability. Numerous domain name registrars, like GoDaddy or Namecheap, allow you to search for available domains. If your first choice is taken, don't fret. You can either try a different TLD or tweak your chosen name slightly. Adding small prefixes or suffixes—such as "get," "my," or "go"—can sometimes open up new possibilities.

Be cautious of trademarks while brainstorming. Using a name that's already trademarked can lead to legal troubles down the road. Before you finalize your choice, conduct a thorough trademark search. Websites like the United States Patent and Trademark Office (USPTO) offer searchable trademark databases that can help you avoid potential conflicts.

While buying a domain, don't fall for upsells. Registrars often offer various additional services like privacy protection, email accounts, and premium DNS. While some of these services might be useful, others are just ways to increase the overall cost. Choose only what you need to get started, and consider scaling your services as your business grows.

Branding is another critical consideration. Your domain name will be a cornerstone of your brand identity. It will appear on your business cards, marketing materials, and social media accounts. Think about how it will look and sound in different contexts. A name might seem clever at first glance, but how will it fare when said out loud during a podcast or at a networking event? Something simple, understandable, and strikingly straightforward is often the best route to take.

Use tools for inspiration. Websites like BustAName or LeanDomainSearch can generate domain name ideas based on your keywords. These tools can help spark creativity and offer combinations you might not have considered. Sometimes, seeing a list of options can push you toward the perfect choice.

Lastly, get feedback. Share your potential domain names with friends, family, or mentors. They can offer a fresh perspective and help you spot issues or point out nuances you might have missed. If your name is confusing to them, it will likely be confusing to your audience as well. Achieving a balance between personal satisfaction and external validation can lead to a more well-rounded choice.

By giving due importance to selecting the right domain name, you're setting a strong foundation for your business website. It's an investment in your brand's future that can pay off significantly in terms of attracting and retaining visitors. So, take your time, weigh all the factors, and choose a domain name that truly represents your vision and ambitions.

CHAPTER 9: CREATING A WEBSITE

Building and Launching Your Site

Once you've secured a domain name that speaks directly to your business's mission and audience, it's time to dive into the exhilarating phase of building and launching your site. This stage bridges the gap between your vision and its digital embodiment, converting ideas into a platform that can captivate and engage customers. The web is your storefront, boardroom, and initial impression, making it a critical component of your entrepreneurial journey.

Getting started on building your website doesn't necessarily require advanced technical skills. Many platforms, like WordPress, Wix, and Shopify, offer user-friendly interfaces with drag-and-drop functionalities. Whether you're selling products, offering services, or simply sharing information, these platforms provide templates that can be customized to fit your brand without writing a single line of code. The key is to choose a platform that aligns with your goals and comfort level.

Your website needs solid infrastructure to run smoothly. Hosting services provide the foundational support that keeps your site online and accessible. Many domain registrars offer hosting services as part of their package, but it's worth exploring other dedicated providers like Bluehost, SiteGround, or HostGator. Look for features such as uptime reliability, scalability, and customer support. For the entrepreneur on a tight schedule, managed hosting services that include maintenance and security can be particularly appealing.

Designing your site should resonate with your brand identity. Consistent colors, typography, and imagery not only help to create a memorable brand but also establish trust and credibility. Simplicity should be your guiding principle; a clean, uncluttered design enhances user experience and makes navigation intuitive. If design isn't your forte, consider hiring a freelance designer. Websites like Upwork and Fiverr are teeming with talented designers who can bring your vision to life without breaking the bank.

Content is king. High-quality content is essential for engaging visitors and converting them into customers. Start by crafting compelling copy that conveys your unique value proposition and speaks directly to your target audience. Be authentic, clear, and persuasive. Include calls-to-action (CTAs) that guide visitors towards taking desired steps, whether that's signing up for a newsletter, making a purchase, or scheduling an appointment.

Search engine optimization (SEO) is another critical component. Optimizing your content for search engines makes it easier for potential customers to find you online. Use relevant keywords naturally within your content, create descriptive meta tags, and ensure your website's structure is search-engine friendly. Tools such as Google Analytics and Yoast SEO can assist in optimizing your site's performance and monitoring its progress.

Beyond the text, multimedia like images, videos, and infographics can make your site more dynamic and engaging. High-resolution images are essential, but make sure they're optimized for web use to avoid slowing down your site. Tutorial videos or customer testimonials can enhance credibility and provide valuable insights into your offerings. Balancing multimedia elements with loading speed is crucial; a slow website can deter potential customers.

Responsive design isn't optional. With an increasing number of users accessing the internet via mobile devices, it is imperative that your site looks and functions well on all screen sizes. Responsive design ensures that your website adapts to various devices, providing a seamless experience whether customers visit from a desktop, tablet, or smartphone. Most modern website builders incorporate mobile-optimization features, but always test your site's responsiveness before launching.

Integrating e-commerce capabilities if you're selling products or services directly from your site involves setting up a secure and user-friendly shopping experience. Platforms like Shopify offer comprehensive tools for managing inventory, processing payments, and tracking orders. Ensure that your payment gateways are secure, providing options like PayPal, Stripe, or direct credit card transactions. Security certificates (SSL) are vital for encrypting data and building trust with your customers.

Prior to launching, rigorously test your site. Check for broken links, ensure forms function correctly, review the site on multiple browsers, and assess performance metrics like loading speed. A soft launch, where a small group of users accesses the site before a full public launch, can provide valuable feedback and uncover issues you might have missed. Encourage this group to

CHAPTER 9: CREATING A WEBSITE

test various functionalities and report back on their experience.

Launching your site doesn't mean the work stops there. In fact, it's just the beginning. Announce your launch across all your marketing channels to generate buzz and drive traffic to your new site. Social media, email campaigns, and collaborations with influencers or bloggers can amplify your reach. Engaging content, regular updates, and ongoing SEO are crucial to maintaining and growing your online presence.

Analytics and user feedback are your best friends post-launch. Utilize tools like Google Analytics to monitor visitor behavior, track key performance indicators, and gather insights that can help you refine your site. Customer feedback is also invaluable. Provide easy ways for visitors to leave reviews and make suggestions, then act on this feedback to continuously improve their experience.

Sharing your journey transparently can humanize your brand and build community. Blog about your experiences, challenges, and triumphs associated with building and launching your site. This not only drives traffic but also fosters a deeper connection with your audience, turning visitors into loyal customers and advocates for your brand.

Ultimately, the process of building and launching your site is an iterative one. It's about creating a dynamic, evolving platform that not only reflects your business today but is adaptable to future growth and change. By implementing these strategies thoughtfully, you'll not only establish a strong online presence but also pave the way for a thriving business. Stay committed to offering value, remain adaptable, and keep the customer at the center of all you do. Your website isn't just a destination; it's a journey worth investing in.

Chapter 10: Social Media Presence

In today's digital age, establishing a robust social media presence is pivotal to rapidly scaling your business and connecting with potential customers. With platforms like Instagram, Facebook, Twitter, and LinkedIn, you can showcase your brand in vibrant and engaging ways, creating a direct line of communication with your audience. Start by identifying which platforms resonate most with your target demographic and focus your efforts there. It's not just about posting content; it's about fostering a community. Engage with your audience through compelling storytelling, regular updates, and responsive interactions. Consistency and authenticity are key. Employ data analytics to understand what's working and refine your strategies accordingly. Remember, your social media profiles are often the first interaction potential customers will have with your brand—make it count.

Setting Up Key Platforms

Social media presence can propel your fledgling business into the spotlight, but it starts with selecting and setting up the right platforms. Let's dive into how you can effectively establish your business on key social media channels to maximize your reach and engagement.

First, understanding the audience you wish to target is crucial. Different social networks cater to different demographics, and knowing who your audience is will guide you in choosing the right platforms. Are you targeting professionals? LinkedIn might be your best bet. Are you looking to grab

CHAPTER 10: SOCIAL MEDIA PRESENCE

the attention of young consumers with engaging visual content? Instagram and TikTok could be where you need to focus. Begin by creating a detailed customer avatar; this will inform your platform choices.

Setting up your profiles means more than just populating the basic fields. Each platform offers a variety of features designed to enhance your presence and credibility. Take the time to fill out your profile completely. Include your business name, a clear and engaging bio, your location, contact information, and a link to your website. On platforms like LinkedIn, don't forget to add your business's achievements, past projects, and any notable clients you've worked with. This builds trust.

Visual identity is paramount on social social media. Select high-quality images and logos that reflect your brand's ethos. Consistency is key; ensure your visual assets are easily recognizable and uniform across all platforms. This not only aids in brand recognition but also presents a professional image. Platforms like Instagram and Facebook are very visual in nature, so use eye-catching images and engage with visual storytelling to draw your audience in.

Next, it's essential to engage with each platform's unique tools and features. Instagram Stories, Facebook Groups, Twitter's trending hashtags, LinkedIn's publishing tools - these are all opportunities to delve deeper into the platform's ecosystem and leverage them for your content. Utilizing these features improves your visibility and boosts engagement. Take the time to learn each feature and consider how it can be integrated into your overall social media strategy.

Creating quality content is where your planning and research come into play. Start by developing a content calendar. This helps in maintaining a consistent posting schedule, which is crucial for keeping your audience engaged. Your content should be a mix of promotional material, industry insights, user-generated content, and personal stories about your entrepreneurial journey. Remember, social media is about building a community and fostering relationships.

Different platforms have varying optimal post lengths and frequencies. For instance, on Twitter, you can post multiple times a day without overwhelming your audience, thanks to its fast-paced nature. However, LinkedIn posts might demand more in-depth content and can be less frequent. Tailoring your content strategy to fit the unique culture of each platform increases your chances of success.

Engaging your audience goes beyond posting content. Interaction is a critical element - respond to comments, answer questions, and join relevant conversations. Show your audience that there's a human behind the brand who values their input. Polls, Q&A sessions, and live videos are excellent ways to engage directly with your audience and create a sense of community.

Analytics are your friend. After running your social media profiles for a while, dive into the analytics tools provided by each platform. These tools offer valuable insights into what's working and what's not. Metrics such as engagement rate, reach, and follower growth can tell you a lot about your audience's preferences and behavior. Use this data to tweak your strategy and optimize your approach continually.

Additionally, automation tools can be game-changers for managing your social media presence efficiently. Tools like Hootsuite, Buffer, and Sprout Social allow you to schedule posts, track analytics, and manage multiple platforms all from one place. While automation can save time, balancing it with authentic, real-time interactions is crucial to avoid coming across as too robotic or disengaged.

Don't underestimate the power of collaborations. Partnering with influencers, bloggers, and other businesses on joint campaigns or shoutouts can significantly amplify your reach. When choosing collaborators, ensure they align with your brand values and appeal to your target audience. A well-executed collaboration can introduce your business to a plethora of potential customers you wouldn't have reached otherwise.

As you build your social media presence, remember that authenticity is key. In a world saturated with content, genuine connections stand out. Don't be afraid to show the behind-the-scenes moments of your entrepreneurial journey, celebrate your milestones, and share the lessons learned from your setbacks. These personal touches resonate deeply with audiences and build a loyal community around your brand.

Finally, remember that building a strong social media presence is a marathon, not a sprint. Consistency, engagement, and authenticity will yield results over time. Stay committed to your strategy, keep refining your approach based on feedback and analytics, and stay genuinely engaged with your audience. Social media is a dynamic landscape, but with the right mindset and tools, it can be a powerful engine for your business's growth and success.

Setting up key platforms effectively can seem daunting, but by breaking it down into achievable steps and focusing on consistency and engagement, you can create a robust social media presence. This presence not only drives immediate business results but sets the foundation for long-term success and growth. Keep experimenting, learning, and adapting, and you'll find that the digital world opens up countless opportunities for your burgeoning venture.

Engaging Your Audience

One of the cornerstones of a successful social media presence is effectively engaging your audience. It goes beyond merely having a large follower count; it's about the quality of interactions, the sense of community you build, and the emotional connection you establish with your followers. When done right, engagement can turn passive followers into loyal customers and brand advocates.

First and foremost, understand the importance of authenticity in your interactions. People are drawn to genuine voices and find value in real conversations. Your business must project an authentic image that resonates with your target audience. This means sharing behind-the-scenes glimpses, making personal connections, and being transparent about your brand's journey. Consider sharing your challenges as well as your successes; this makes you more relatable and trustworthy.

Make sure to actively listen to what your audience is saying. Social media is not a one-way street; it's a platform for dialogues. Pay attention to comments, messages, and mentions. Responding promptly and thoughtfully to these interactions not only shows that you value their input but also fosters a sense of community. Your followers will appreciate that you take time out to hear their concerns and viewpoints, creating a more loyal and engaged audience.

Interactive content can play a huge role in engaging your followers. Polls, Q&A sessions, and live videos are excellent ways to make your audience feel involved and valued. Such formats encourage immediate feedback and participation, providing insights into what your audience loves or needs. For example, hosting a live session to discuss new product features or industry trends can bring a surge of engagement and give you real-time feedback.

Consistency is another critical element. Regular posting keeps your brand at the forefront of your audience's mind, ensuring you remain relevant. However, it's not just about frequency but also about maintaining a consistent voice and style. Your posts should reflect your brand's identity, whether that's fun and quirky or formal and informative. This consistency builds a cohesive image and makes it easier for your audience to identify and connect with your brand.

A good engagement strategy is also grounded in value. Every post you make should provide some sort of benefit to your followers, whether it's educational, entertaining, or thought-provoking. Quality content that adds value will naturally attract interactions. Share useful tips, interesting insights, and valuable resources. The aim is to become a go-to resource for your followers, something they look forward to seeing in their feed.

Don't underestimate the power of storytelling in engaging your audience. People love stories because they're memorable and emotionally impactful. Share stories about your brand, your team, and your customers. Highlight user-generated content to show real-world applications and benefits of your product or service. Stories can make complex ideas easier to understand and help establish an emotional connection with your audience.

Leverage social proof to increase engagement. Testimonials, reviews, and case studies are compelling as they provide third-party validation of your brand. When followers see that others have had positive experiences with your products or services, they're more likely to engage with your content and trust your brand. Consider creating posts that highlight these testimonials or share customer success stories to build credibility.

Contests and giveaways are also powerful tools for engagement. They not only reward your followers for their participation but also generate buzz around your brand. When planning these, make sure the rules are simple and the prizes are relevant to your audience. Promoting the contest across various platforms can help attract a broader audience and increase overall engagement.

Monitoring and analytics are essential to understanding engagement effectiveness. Utilize social media analytics tools to track metrics like comments, shares, likes, and impressions. These metrics will provide insights into what types of content resonate most with your audience. Use these insights to refine your strategies, experimenting with different types of posts and interactions to see what works best.

Collaborate with influencers and other brands to broaden your reach and improve engagement. Influencers have established relationships with their followers, and when they endorse your brand, it can lead to higher engagement. Partner with influencers who align with your brand values and target audience to ensure the collaboration is impactful and genuine. Similarly, collaborating with other brands can introduce you to a new audience and provide mutual benefits in terms of engagement and exposure.

Timely engagement can also leverage current events and trending topics. Being part of the conversation around these events can make your brand more relevant and relatable. However, it's crucial to ensure that your participation in such discussions aligns with your brand values and does not come across as opportunistic. Adding thoughtful commentary or unique takes on trending topics can enhance your brand's visibility and engagement.

Encourage your audience to engage with your content by asking questions and prompting discussions. Simple questions at the end of a post can stimulate comments and conversations. "What do you think?" or "Have you tried this?" can be enough to get your followers talking and interacting with your content. Providing clear calls to action in your posts also directs your audience on how to engage, whether it's sharing a post, clicking a link, or tagging a friend.

Finally, never ignore negative comments or feedback. Addressing them head-on can show that you care about all of your followers' opinions and are willing to make necessary improvements. Responding to criticism in a calm and constructive manner can often turn a negative experience into a positive one, showcasing your commitment to customer satisfaction.

In conclusion, engaging your audience on social media requires a blend of authenticity, consistency, and value-driven content. It's not about amassing a large number of followers quickly, but about fostering genuine relationships and building a community around your brand. Each interaction holds the potential to convert followers into loyal customers and advocates for your business, bringing you one step closer to that million-dollar success.

Chapter 11: Product Development

Developing a product quickly doesn't mean cutting corners; it means being agile and focused on what truly matters. Start with a clear vision and translate that into a rapid prototype—it's easier than you might think with today's tools. Time is of the essence here; gather feedback as soon as your prototype hits the ground. Use that feedback to iterate swiftly, refining your product into something your target audience genuinely wants. Remember, it's better to have a functional product in the hands of consumers than a perfect one still in development. Be resilient and adaptable—every bit of feedback is a stepping stone to your next iteration. The goal is to perfect the product iteratively, learning and evolving with each step to meet market demand efficiently and effectively.

Prototyping Quickly

Speed is the name of the game when it comes to prototyping, especially if you're aiming to launch a million-dollar business in just 48 hours. Your primary focus should be on creating a functional model of your product that solves a real problem for customers. Prototyping quickly allows you to test your assumptions, gather early feedback, and pivot if necessary, all within a short timeframe.

The first step in rapid prototyping is to distill your idea down to its core elements. Ask yourself, "What are the must-have features that will make this product usable and valuable to customers?" These features should be your focus. If you're building an app, for example, it doesn't need to be fully polished or feature-rich at this stage. Users should be able to achieve the main goal of the app without unnecessary extras that could slow you down.

Consider leveraging no-code and low-code platforms, especially if you're not tech-savvy. These platforms can help you design and deploy functional applications within hours. Tools like Bubble, Adalo, and Glide can be incredibly useful for creating web apps or mobile apps quickly. The advantage here is that you won't have to rely on a developer, which saves both time and money.

Physical products hinge on a slightly different approach but can still be prototyped rapidly. If your product is more tangible, such as a consumer good, there's a wide range of prototyping kits available. Basic supplies like 3D printers, Arduino boards for electronics, and laser cutters can help you whip up a prototype in your garage or home office. Even if these tools are not within your budget, local maker spaces and fab labs often offer access to these technologies for a small fee.

Another valuable resource in quick prototyping is the concept of Minimum Viable Product (MVP). The MVP is a version of your product with just enough features to satisfy early adopters. Gather as much customer feedback as possible from this version to guide further development. Your MVP doesn't need to be perfect; it needs to be functional and testable. The key is to understand what aspects of the product resonate with users and what can be improved.

Feedback is crucial at this stage. Utilize online surveys, focus groups, or even simple social media polls to gather intelligence. Don't be afraid to ask your personal network for their input. Sometimes, a fresh pair of eyes can spot potential issues or opportunities that you've overlooked.

Remember, the goal here is to build, measure, and learn. The faster you can iterate through this cycle, the closer you'll get to a product that truly adds value to your customers' lives. A simple paper prototype or wireframe can be extremely effective for digital products, allowing you to test user flows and interactions without committing to code.

Let's talk a bit about the tools to streamline this process. Online platforms like Figma or Sketch are excellent for creating user interfaces and getting immediate feedback. For those needing something more tactile, a mix of Post-it notes, cardboard, and glue can often bring your vision to life quickly and effectively.

Outsourcing can also be part of your rapid prototyping strategy. Websites like Fiverr, Upwork, and Freelancer allow you to hire experts for specific tasks, from design to coding. This way, you can focus on your core business activities and leave specialized tasks to professionals. Choose freelancers with high ratings and ensure you communicate your vision clearly to get the best results.

While prototyping is a major step, don't overlook the importance of documenting everything. Keep a log of your assumptions, what you tested, and the feedback received. This data will be invaluable as you refine your product and prepare for launch. Good documentation also makes it easier to bring other team members or investors up to speed.

When it comes to iterating, don't be afraid to make bold changes based on customer feedback. If an aspect of your product isn't resonating, it's better to find out early and pivot than to stick to an idea that won't succeed. This willingness to adapt can be the difference between success and failure, especially within the tight timeframe of 48 hours.

Prototyping quickly doesn't mean cutting corners on quality. Your prototype needs to be functional enough to demonstrate its value but also sturdy enough to withstand initial use. Think of it as building a strong foundation; its solidity will support future enhancements.

Lastly, keep the end goal in sight: a working prototype that solves a customer's problem. This clear focus will guide you through the chaos of a short development cycle. By maintaining clarity on your primary objectives, you'll navigate the rapid prototyping phase with agility and effectiveness.

In conclusion, a quick prototype is the cornerstone of a rapid business launch. By focusing on essential features, leveraging available tools, gathering feedback, and being ready to iterate, you'll set a strong foundation for your business. The insights you gather during this phase will inform your next steps and guide you toward creating a product that not only meets but exceeds customer expectations. Ultimately, the ability to prototype quickly is a skill that will serve you well beyond the initial 48 hours, setting the stage for continuous innovation and growth.

Iterating Based on Feedback

When it comes to creating a successful product, your first version is rarely going to be your last. This is where the practice of iterating based on feedback becomes essential. It's not just about tweaking the product—it's about understanding your customer, the market, and aligning your offering to meet evolving needs and expectations. Iteration is a cycle of improvement that, done correctly, can turn a good product into a great one.

The first step in this iterative process is collecting feedback. Feedback comes from various sources—customers, beta testers, your sales team, and even online reviews. Actively seek it out and make it easy for people to provide. Use surveys, social media polls, and direct questions to get a pulse on what's working and what's not. Be specific in your queries. Asking questions like, "What feature do you find the least useful?" or "How can we improve your experience?" can yield insights you might not have considered.

Once you have the feedback, the challenge is to categorize and analyze it. Not all feedback will be equally valuable, and some of it may even contradict other pieces. Separate the feedback into categories such as usability issues, feature requests, and bug reports. This will help you prioritize which areas need immediate attention and which can be scheduled for later updates. Employing tools like spreadsheets or specialized software can aid in managing this data efficiently.

Analyzing feedback involves identifying patterns and recurring issues. If multiple users are reporting the same problem, it's a red flag that needs immediate attention. Sometimes, the feedback might not be straightforward, requiring you to read between the lines. For instance, if users say they find a certain feature "confusing," you might need to dig deeper to understand whether it's a design flaw, poor instructions, or just a misplaced button. It's crucial to transform this qualitative feedback into quantitative action points.

Iteration isn't just about making changes; it's about making informed changes. Once you've identified the areas for improvement, it's time to brainstorm and plan your revisions. Involve your team in this process for a more diverse set of ideas and solutions. Conducting a brainstorming session with different departments can unveil unique perspectives and innovative solutions. Be open to radical changes but also careful not to overcomplicate the product.

Before rolling out any changes, it's wise to test them. Implementing A/B tests can be highly effective, allowing you to compare the performance of your original version with the updated one. This way, you have data to support whether a change has genuinely improved the user experience. Testing ensures that you're not replacing one problem with another.

Communication is key throughout this iterative process. Keep your team updated on the changes and the reasons behind them. Transparency fosters a culture of continuous improvement and engages everyone in the mission. Also, keep your customers in the loop. Let them know that their feedback is being acted upon and that their voices matter. This not only builds trust but also encourages more constructive feedback in the future.

After implementing the changes, the cycle doesn't end—it starts anew. Continuous monitoring and gathering feedback should become ingrained in your product development culture. Set regular intervals to revisit feedback and measure the impact of your changes. Track metrics like customer satisfaction scores, churn rates, and feature engagement to gauge success. Doing so ensures that your product consistently evolves to meet the market's demands.

Iteration based on feedback can sometimes feel like an endless loop, but it's a vital part of staying relevant. The market is ever-changing, competitors are always catching up, and customer expectations are never static. By continuously collecting feedback and iterating your product, you stay one step ahead. This commitment to ongoing improvement can be a decisive factor in a product's long-term success.

Remember, perfection is a moving target. Your goal shouldn't be to reach a 'perfect' product but to keep moving towards an ever-improving one. The beauty of iteration is that it allows you to make consistent, incremental improvements over time. Each iteration builds on the last, creating a robust, resilient product that can adapt to new challenges and opportunities.

In conclusion, iterating based on feedback is more than just a practice; it's a mindset. It requires a willingness to listen, adapt, and grow. It's about fostering a culture of continuous improvement where every piece of feedback is a potential stepping stone to greatness. For side hustlers, business owners, and entrepreneurs, mastering the art of iteration can be the difference between fleeting success and sustained achievement.

Ultimately, it's a journey of learning and adapting, driven by the very people who matter most—your customers. So, embrace their feedback, iterate with intention, and watch your product evolve into something truly extraordinary.

Chapter 12: Pricing Strategies

Mastering pricing strategies can make or break your million-dollar business concept, especially when you're working with a 48-hour launch window. To strike the perfect balance, you've got to start by calculating your costs and margins, ensuring you're not just covering expenses but also generating profit. Dive deep into understanding the market landscape and establishing competitive prices without undervaluing your offerings. Remember, your pricing strategy isn't just about numbers—it's a direct reflection of your brand's value proposition. By aligning your pricing with your target audience's expectations and your overall business goals, you can position your product or service effectively and maximize your chances for rapid success. Pricing isn't set in stone; be open to tweaking your prices based on customer feedback and market shifts, ensuring you're always ahead of the curve.

Calculating Costs and Margins

Getting your pricing right is crucial. But before you can even think about pricing, you need to understand your costs and margins. These numbers will tell you whether your business idea is viable and profitable in the long run.

Start by identifying all your costs. There are two main types to consider: fixed costs and variable costs. Fixed costs are the ones that don't change regardless of how much you sell. Things like rent, salaries, and insurance fall into this category. Variable costs, on the other hand, fluctuate with your level of production or sales. These might include materials, shipping, and commission fees.

Make a comprehensive list of your fixed costs. This will give you a baseline number that you need to cover each month. Don't underestimate these costs; forgetting even one or two minor expenses can throw off your entire calculation. Think about everything from utilities to office supplies and make sure each one is accounted for.

Next, calculate your variable costs on a per-unit basis. For example, if you're selling custom-made t-shirts, figure out the cost of fabric, printing, and packaging per shirt. This step is essential for understanding how much each sale will add to your bottom line, or if it might actually be costing you more than it's worth.

Once you've got a handle on your costs, it's time to look at your margins. Your margin is what you have left after covering your costs, and it can be calculated as a percentage of your selling price. The formula is simple:

Gross Margin = (Selling Price - Cost of Goods Sold) / Selling Price

The gross margin percentage will give you a clear idea of how much you're making on each sale. If your margins are too slim, it might be difficult to scale your business or even stay afloat.

Understanding and calculating your break-even point is another critical step. This is the number of units you need to sell to cover all your costs. To find this, divide your total fixed costs by the difference between your selling price and variable costs per unit. The formula looks like this:

Break-Even Point = Fixed Costs / (Selling Price - Variable Costs)

Knowing your break-even point gives you a target to aim for. It helps you set realistic sales goals and gauge the initial success of your business. If you find that your break-even point is unattainable, it might be time to re-evaluate either your costs or your pricing strategy.

Your profit margin is another pivotal metric. While the gross margin tells you what you are making on each product, the profit margin will show your net profitability across the business. The formula is:

Profit Margin = (Net Profit / Total Revenue) * 100

This percentage helps you understand how well your business converts sales into actual profit. It incorporates all your costs, both fixed and variable,

CHAPTER 12: PRICING STRATEGIES

and gives a more holistic view of your financial health.

While calculating these numbers, you should also consider indirect costs—expenses that aren't directly tied to a sale but still affect your bottom line. These could include marketing costs, administrative expenses, and even software subscriptions. Ignoring these can lead to a distorted view of profitability.

It's not just about crunching numbers; it's also about regularly reviewing and adjusting them. Markets change, vendor prices fluctuate, and your business evolves. Periodically revisiting your costs and margins ensures that you're always making informed decisions based on current data.

Another important aspect to consider is contribution margin, which is essentially the selling price per unit minus the variable cost per unit. This differs from gross margin and is crucial for decision-making processes, especially when planning for short-term financial tasks.

Contribution Margin = Selling Price - Variable Costs

This metric helps in understanding how much product sales contribute to the fixed costs, and eventually, to the profit. Tracking this can provide insights into which products are the most profitable and can guide you in tailoring your product mix.

Automated tools and software can simplify tracking these numbers. Programs like QuickBooks, FreshBooks, and even Excel spreadsheets can help you keep an accurate account of all your expenses and revenues. Utilizing technology can not only save time but also minimize errors, ensuring that your calculations are precise.

Negotiating with suppliers is another way to improve your margins. If you're able to get a better deal on raw materials or shipping costs, those savings will directly impact your profitability. Building strong relationships with your vendors and regularly revisiting contracts can yield long-term benefits.

Don't shy away from outsourcing tasks that can be done more cost-effectively by someone else. Whether it's accounting, marketing, or even manufacturing, outsourcing can sometimes reduce your variable costs. However, always weigh the quality against the cost to ensure you're making a wise decision.

You should also consider economies of scale. As your production increases, the cost per unit often decreases. This can substantially improve your margin if managed correctly. Planning for scalable solutions from the outset can set you up for greater profitability as your business grows.

While most of this might sound complex, the core idea is to ensure that every product or service you sell contributes positively to your financial health. The objective is not just to cover your costs but also to ensure that your margins are robust enough to support reinvestment, growth, and a safety net for tough times.

Finally, remember: calculating costs and margins isn't a one-time activity. It's an ongoing process that demands your attention. Keep refining your numbers, and you'll have a solid foundation for setting a pricing strategy that fuels your business's growth and success. Consistency in reviewing these calculations can be the difference between a thriving business and one that struggles to break even.

Mastering the art of calculating costs and margins equips you with the knowledge necessary to make data-driven decisions confidently. And in the fast-paced world of side hustles and startups, this knowledge is your competitive edge.

Establishing Competitive Prices

In the race to build a million-dollar business in just 48 hours, setting the right price for your product or service can make all the difference. It's more than just a number; it's a signal to your customers, a reflection of your brand, and a critical factor that determines your profitability. Establishing competitive prices is an art that requires a blend of market research, psychological understanding, and strategic thinking.

When determining your pricing, the first step is to understand your costs. This might seem straightforward, but it's essential to delve into both direct and indirect costs. Direct costs include materials, labor, and production expenses. Indirect costs encompass overheads such as rent, utilities, and even marketing efforts. Overlooking these can lead to underpricing, squeezing your margins and making it difficult to sustain your new venture.

Once you've grasped your cost structure, it's time to look outward. Competitor analysis is crucial in crafting competitive prices. This involves scrutinizing the pricing strategies of businesses offering similar products or services. What price points are they hitting? Are they discounting or offering premium options? By understanding the landscape, you can identify gaps and opportunities that differentiate your pricing strategy.

Moreover, pricing isn't just about matching the competition. It's about positioning your product in the market. Premium pricing might imply luxury and exclusivity, while lower prices can attract bargain hunters seeking value. Decide where you want to position your brand and adjust your pricing accordingly. For instance, if your product quality is unmatched, commanding a higher price could justify the superior value you provide.

It's essential to avoid a one-size-fits-all strategy. Different customer segments may value the same product differently. To leverage this, consider adopting a tiered pricing strategy. Offer a basic, mid-range, and premium version of your product. Each tier should cater to distinct customer needs and perceived value. This not only expands your market but also maximizes revenue from diverse segments.

Psychology plays a significant role in pricing. Consumers' perceptions of value can be influenced by subtle differences in price presentation. For example, pricing something at $9.99 instead of $10.00 can make it seem significantly cheaper. The concept of "left-digit effect," where consumers focus more on the left-most digits, is a powerful tool. Pay attention to these nuances to refine your pricing strategy.

Discount strategies can drive both initial sales and long-term loyalty. However, they require careful management. Frequent deep discounts can erode perceived value and create expectations for low prices, harming profitability in the long run. Instead, consider limited-time promotions, bundle deals, or loyalty rewards that add value without diminishing your brand's worth. This approach can spur urgency and repeat business without creating a dependency on discounts.

Early pricing adjustments are another tactic to consider. When you first launch, you might not hit the ideal price point on the first try. This is where agile pricing comes into play. Monitor sales, customer feedback, and market reactions closely. Don't be afraid to make incremental adjustments based on real-time data. This iterative approach ensures you stay competitive and profitable as your business evolves.

Another tactic worth exploring is value-based pricing. Here, you set prices based on the perceived value to the customer rather than just costs or competitor prices. This requires a deep understanding of your customers' needs and the unique benefits your product offers. Conducting surveys, focus groups, and customer interviews can provide insights into what your target market is willing to pay and why.

Subscription models can also be a game-changer, especially for services. They provide recurring revenue and foster customer loyalty. Determine whether a monthly or annual subscription aligns better with your business model and customer preferences. Offering a discounted rate for longer-term commitments can also ensure a steady cash flow and increase customer retention rates.

For products, dynamic pricing might be a suitable strategy. This involves adjusting prices based on demand, time of day, or market conditions. E-commerce platforms often use algorithms to automatically adjust prices based on these factors. While it's more complex to manage, dynamic pricing can optimize revenue by ensuring you're neither underselling during peak demand times nor overpricing in slower periods.

Lastly, communication of pricing is key. How you present your prices can significantly impact customer perception and purchasing decisions. Ensure your pricing structure is transparent and easily understandable. Highlight the benefits clearly associated with each price point. If you're offering a high-value service, break down the costs so customers see where their money is going and feel the value they're receiving.

Establishing competitive prices is ultimately about balance. It requires a harmonization of cost structures, market analysis, customer insights, and strategic pricing models. By mastering this balance, you position your business not only to attract customers but to do so in a way that's sustainable and profitable. The goal isn't just to make sales, but to build a financial foundation that supports growth and scalability.

Remember, pricing is both art and science. It's about numbers, but it's also about understanding human behavior, market dynamics, and brand positioning. Stay flexible, continuously gather feedback, and be ready to adapt. By doing so, you'll not only establish competitive prices but lay the groundwork for a thriving business that stands the test of time.

Chapter 13: Marketing and Sales Plan

To catapult your business to the million-dollar mark within 48 hours, a robust marketing and sales plan is indispensable. Start by crafting a compelling message that clearly communicates the unique value your product or service offers. It's crucial to know exactly who you're speaking to and tailor your message to resonate with your target audience. Next, strategically choose your marketing channels—whether it's social media, email campaigns, or influencer partnerships, select platforms where your audience spends the most time. Balancing low-cost, high-impact tactics with paid advertising can maximize your reach without breaking the bank. Remember, your goal is to engage potential customers quickly and convert that interest into sales with irresistible offers and persuasive sales funnels. Think of your marketing and sales efforts as the engine oil that keeps your business running smoothly and efficiently, propelling you toward rapid growth and success.

Welcome to the heart of your marketing and sales plan—

Crafting Your Message

In the whirlwind journey to turn your side hustle into a million-dollar business, crafting your message is quintessential. Think of your message as the soul of your brand; it's what connects you to your audience on a deep, emotional level. It's not just about what you're saying, but how, when, and where you're saying it. Let's delve into building a compelling message that resonates and drives action.

First off, you need to know your audience inside and out. Who are they? What are their pain points? What keeps them up at night? An intimate understanding of your audience will steer your messaging and make it profoundly compelling. Whether it's students cramming for exams or stay-at-home parents looking to earn extra income, your message should strike a chord that resonates.

Human beings are wired to respond to stories. Your message should tell a story—one that your audience not only listens to but one they see themselves in. Share your journey, your struggles, and your victories. Did you start with a simple idea over a weekend and turn it into something incredible? Let them know. Your authenticity will make your brand relatable, believable, and unforgettable.

It's important to keep your messaging concise and clear. Time is precious, and attention spans are short. You've got mere seconds to engage your audience, so every word must count. Translate complex ideas into simple, digestible bites. Avoid jargon and speak in your audience's language. A powerful elevator pitch can work wonders—aim to communicate who you are, what you're offering, and why it matters in thirty seconds or less.

Consider your unique selling proposition (USP). What sets you apart from the crowd? Your USP is the backbone of your message and will help you stand out in a saturated market. Maybe you offer a unique product or exceptional customer service. Highlight these distinctions in your messaging. For example, if your product is eco-friendly, focus on how your audience can help the planet by choosing your brand.

Another crucial element is emotional appeal. People make decisions based on emotion and justify them with logic. Your message should tap into the emotional triggers of your audience. Are they seeking peace of mind, happiness, convenience, or perhaps prestige? Use emotive language and imagery that align with these desires. The goal is to create an emotional bond that makes your brand memorable.

Consistency is key. Your message should be uniform across all channels—whether it's your website, social media, or email campaigns. Inconsistencies can confuse your audience and dilute your brand. Develop a brand voice that encapsulates your identity and values, and ensure it's reflected across every piece of content. This sense of uniformity builds trust and reinforces your brand.

Leverage testimonials and reviews. Social proof is an influential tool in your messaging arsenal. When potential customers see that others have had positive experiences with your brand, it lends credibility and accelerates the decision-making process. Highlight testimonials prominently in your communications. A message backed by real-world endorsements is far more persuasive.

Visual elements also play a significant role in crafting your message. Humans are visual creatures; we process images faster than text. Use compelling visuals that align with your brand's message. Whether it's a sleek logo, professional product photos, or engaging infographics, ensure your visuals are high-quality and consistent with your brand identity.

Segment your audience for targeted messaging. Not all customers are the same, so a one-size-fits-all approach won't cut it. By segmenting your audience based on demographics, behaviors, or preferences, you can craft tailored messages that speak directly to each group's unique needs and motivations. This level of personalization can significantly enhance engagement and conversion rates.

Timing matters. Even the most compelling message can fall flat if delivered at the wrong time. Understand your audience's behaviors and craft your messaging schedule accordingly. When are they most active on social media? When do they check their emails? Align your message delivery with these peak times to maximize impact.

In today's digital era, interactivity can elevate your messaging game. Encourage your audience to engage with your brand through interactive content like polls, quizzes, and live videos. This two-way interaction can deepen your audience's connection to your brand and provide valuable insights into their preferences and behaviors.

Don't shy away from tweaking and evolving your message based on feedback and performance metrics. The market is dynamic, and so should be your messaging. Use analytics to track what's working and what's not, and be

CHAPTER 13: MARKETING AND SALES PLAN

agile enough to make the necessary adjustments. Continuous improvement and iteration will keep your message relevant and effective.

Remember, simplicity is often the ultimate sophistication. A simple, clear, and heartfelt message can resonate far more than a convoluted, overly clever one. Sometimes, the best way to connect with your audience is by getting straight to the point and speaking from the heart.

Your message should embody the essence of your brand, reflecting its mission, vision, and values. It's the guiding light that will attract your audience, retain their interest, and compel them to act. Crafting it thoughtfully and strategically is non-negotiable if you aim to convert a fleeting weekend idea into a sustainable, thriving business.

Crafting your message is not a one-time task but an ongoing journey. As your business grows and evolves, so should your message. Stay tuned to your audience's needs, market trends, and your own business milestones. With a well-crafted message, you're not just selling a product or service; you're offering an experience, a solution, and a promise. That's the real magic of impactful messaging.

Choosing Marketing Channels

Choosing the right marketing channels is like finding the best highways to get you to your destination efficiently. It's not just about getting your business out there; it's about getting your business in front of the right audience. For budding entrepreneurs and side hustlers, especially those launching a business within an ambitious 48-hour timeframe, choosing the right marketing channels can make all the difference between hitting the ground running and stumbling at the starting line.

So, what exactly are marketing channels? In simple terms, these are the avenues through which you can deliver your marketing messages to potential customers. Think of them as bridges that connect you to your audience. They can be online or offline, ranging from social media platforms to traditional media like TV and radio. The trick lies in identifying which channels your target audience frequents and how they prefer to consume information.

One of the most cost-effective and accessible channels to tap into initially is social media. Platforms like Facebook, Instagram, Twitter, and LinkedIn offer a multifaceted approach to reaching different demographics. Facebook is extensive and versatile, perfect for targeting a broad audience with its robust advertising options. Instagram captures a younger, more visually driven crowd, which is ideal if your product has strong visual appeal. Twitter allows for real-time interaction and engagement, making it great for customer service and trending topics. LinkedIn, on the other hand, is the platform of choice for professionals and B2B marketing.

For those who prefer to connect on a more personal level, email marketing remains one of the most powerful tools in your arsenal. Building an email list might take a bit of effort, but it pays off in the long run. Emails allow for direct communication with your audience, and when crafted well, they can drive significant engagement and conversions. Tools like MailChimp and Constant Contact make managing email campaigns easy, even for beginners.

Another powerful yet often overlooked channel is content marketing. This doesn't just mean starting a blog—although that's a solid option—it encompasses anything that provides value and engages your audience. Content marketing includes videos, infographics, podcasts, webinars, and eBooks. The beauty of this approach lies in its versatility and longevity; good content can continue to attract and engage customers long after it's initially created.

Search engine optimization (SEO) should also be part of your marketing strategy. SEO helps your business appear in search engine results when potential customers are looking for products or services like yours. While SEO is a long-term strategy, it is crucial for organic growth. Tools like Google's Keyword Planner and SEMrush can help you identify the most effective keywords to target.

Paid advertising, whether through Google AdWords or social media ads, can give your business the immediate visibility boost it needs, especially in those critical early days post-launch. While this requires a budget, platforms typically offer detailed targeting options to ensure your ads reach the people most likely to be interested in your business. Be sure to test different ad formats and messages to see what resonates best with your audience.

Offline channels shouldn't be ignored either. Traditional media, such as print advertising, radio, and television, can still be effective, especially when used in conjunction with online marketing. Local newspaper ads, flyers, and posters can be particularly effective for businesses targeting a local audience. Networking events, trade shows, and community gatherings offer invaluable opportunities for face-to-face promotion.

Influencer marketing is another consideration. You don't need to target celebrities with millions of followers. Micro-influencers, who have smaller but highly engaged audiences, can offer a more affordable and effective way to reach potential customers. The key here is authenticity; an endorsement from an influencer who genuinely believes in your product can carry a lot of weight.

Remember, not all marketing channels will be suitable for every business. A service-based business might benefit more from content marketing and SEO, while a product-oriented business could see quicker results with social media and paid ads. The goal should be to select a mix of channels that complement each other and align with your business objectives.

Finally, whichever channels you choose, tracking and analytics are essential. Utilize tools like Google Analytics, social media insights, and CRM systems to monitor the effectiveness of your campaigns. Keeping an eye on metrics such as engagement rate, click-through rate, and conversion rate will help you refine your approach and make data-driven decisions.

In conclusion, choosing the right marketing channels is less about casting a wide net and more about making strategic choices based on where your audience is and how they prefer to engage. It's a blend of science and art—requiring both analytics and intuition. You won't get it perfect right out of the gate, but with continuous assessment and adaptation, you'll find the right mix that works for your business. And remember, the best marketing plan is one that's as dynamic and adaptable as the ever-changing landscape in which you're operating.

Chapter 14: Launch Day Strategy

It's finally here—Launch Day! The key to a successful launch lies in meticulous preparation and flawless execution. Start by making sure every aspect of your business is ready for its debut: from your website being fully functional to your social media accounts primed and your product polished to perfection. In anticipation of the big day, engage with your audience through teasers, countdowns, and sneak peeks that build excitement and curiosity. Coordinate your team, ensuring everyone knows their role and responsibilities. On launch day, focus on creating a buzz—mobilize your supporters, push out a well-timed press release, and harness the power of influencers who resonate with your target market. Keep the momentum going by closely monitoring feedback and making real-time adjustments. Remember, the goal isn't just to make a splash but to create waves that sustain your business's growth long after the launch.

Preparing for Launch

So, you've done the groundwork: brainstorming, researching, branding, all checked off your list. Now, as we edge closer to the most exciting day yet—launch day—it's crucial to make sure all elements are in place. The preparation phase can make or break your launch. Let's dive into how to set yourself up for maximum impact.

Before anything else, your first order of business is to conduct a final audit of your product or service. This means going through every aspect with a fine-tooth comb. Are all your logistics in place? For instance, if you're launching a physical product, make sure your inventory is sufficient to meet the initial surge of orders. Ensure your supply chain is rock-solid and there are no potential bottlenecks that could derail your launch day. Equally, for a digital product, scrutinize every feature. It might be helpful to run another round of beta testing with a fresh set of eyes to catch anything you might have missed. Don't underestimate this step; it's your last line of defense against unforeseen issues.

As you lock in your final product details, turn your attention to the customer touchpoints. These include your website, social media presence, and customer service channels. Test every button, link, and form on your website. Ensure that everything is functional, from the payment gateway to the confirmation emails. You don't want potential customers abandoning their shopping carts because of a technical glitch. First impressions matter, and a seamless user experience can significantly influence your launch's success.

Parallel to these checks, consider communication strategy. Reach out to your early adopters and current followers. A well-crafted email or social media post that hints at something big coming up can build anticipation. People love being in the know, and giving your community a sneak peek or even a launch-exclusive discount can do wonders. Generate a buzz that's palpable—make your impending launch the talk of the town, or at least of your niche market. Remember, urgency and exclusivity can often tip the scales in your favor.

Speaking of generating buzz, focus on influencer and media outreach. Collaborate with influencers relevant to your industry to preview your product or service to their audience. Influencers can amplify your reach far beyond what you could achieve alone. They bring a level of trust and authenticity that resonates deeply with their followers. Draft press releases tailored to different media outlets. Personalize your pitches to journalists, bloggers, and media personalities who would find your story compelling. Whether it's a unique product, an inspirational startup story, or an innovative service—find the angle that makes your launch newsworthy.

To complement your media efforts, gear up for a robust social media campaign. Schedule posts that build up to your launch, each adding to the anticipation. Use a mix of content—teaser videos, countdown timers, behind-the-scenes looks, and customer testimonials. Employ hashtags to increase visibility, and don't shy away from live streaming on platforms like Instagram or Facebook. A live Q&A session on the eve of the launch can provide that final push and engage your audience directly. The goal is to create a cohesive narrative that speaks to your brand's ethos and builds excitement.

Transitioning from marketing to practical preparations, ensure your team is prepped and ready. Even if you're a one-person operation, having a clear launch day plan matters. Outline each step, from the moment you make the website live to the first order confirmation email. If you have a team, conduct a brief meeting to go over everyone's roles and responsibilities. Set clear expectations and contingency plans for potential hiccups. Being prepared for any scenario will keep you cool under pressure, ensuring a smoother launch day.

Let's not forget customer service. Equip your customer support team with all the necessary information and tools. Draft cheat sheets with common questions and answers, ensuring everyone from your social media manager to your customer service rep is on the same page. The first 24 hours will set the tone for your brand's customer relations. Quick, informed, and friendly responses can turn potential hiccups into opportunities for exceptional customer service. Your readiness can convert those first-time buyers into long-term loyal customers.

Financial readiness also deserves a mention. Double-check your pricing strategies, ensuring they align with your marketing and financial goals. Make sure you're ready to implement any special launch discounts or bundles. Concurrently, keep your payment processing system on alert for any anomalies. The last thing you want is to deal with payment issues just as you're gaining momentum. Streamlining these details now can save you headaches later.

Another overlooked but immensely important element is psychological preparation. Get your mind in the right space. Launching can be chaotic, the culmination of weeks, if not months, of hard work. Maintain a positive yet realistic mindset. There will be highs and lows—celebrate each small victory

CHAPTER 14: LAUNCH DAY STRATEGY

but be prepared to address and learn from any setbacks swiftly. Breathing exercises, meditation, or even a brief walk can help clear your mind and focus your energy.

Finally, conduct a simulation of your launch day. This might sound over-the-top, but a dry run can reveal unanticipated issues. Is your website handling the load? How quickly can your team process an influx of orders or inquiries? A simulated launch day helps spotlight potential weaknesses and allows you to address them proactively. Each member of your team, or each aspect of your solo operation, should be tested to ensure everything operates flawlessly.

With all these elements prepared meticulously, you're setting the stage for a launch day that could redefine your entrepreneurial journey. The groundwork you lay now will support not just the initial burst of activity, but the sustained growth and success of your venture. This is your moment to make the biggest splash possible—so take that deep breath, double-check your list, and get ready to marvel at the magic of a well-executed launch. Here's to your future success!

Executing the Launch

The morning of your launch isn't the time for second-guessing. Remember, you've spent countless hours preparing for this very moment. Every decision, no matter how small, has led you to this point. You've validated your idea, built your brand, and prepared your marketing strategy. Now, it's all about execution and seizing the opportunity.

Start by taking a deep breath and reviewing your day's schedule. You've likely crafted a detailed launch plan, including specific tasks, timelines, and assigned responsibilities. Refer back to this plan often to ensure everything is on track. Don't hesitate to delegate tasks to team members or trusted confidants; remember, a successful launch is rarely a solo endeavor. Rally your team and inspire them to share in your vision. This moment is as much theirs as it is yours.

Stagger your announcements and updates across different platforms.

Launching on social media? Consider using live features like Facebook Live, Instagram Stories, or even a YouTube premiere. These tools give your audience real-time engagement opportunities, heightening excitement and driving immediate traffic to your website or sales page. This isn't just about selling a product; it's about creating a moment, a memory. Your goal is to make your launch day an event that people talk about.

Use email marketing to its fullest potential. Have you built an email list from your pre-launch activities? Now's the time to use it. Draft an engaging, visually appealing launch email with clear calls to action. Personalize your emails as much as possible to make each recipient feel like a VIP. Include special launch day offers or limited-time discounts to create urgency. The open rates on launch day will significantly impact your initial sales—so ensure your email content is compelling and your headlines are irresistible.

Monitor your website analytics throughout the day. Frequently check metrics like visitor counts, bounce rates, and conversion rates. This real-time data will help you identify what's working and what isn't. For example, if you notice a high bounce rate from a particular traffic source, it might be worth investigating and tweaking your message or offer for that audience. Don't be afraid to pivot if something isn't working. Being adaptable and responsive can be the difference between a good launch and a great one.

Social proof and testimonials can also be game-changers. As orders come in, encourage your early customers to leave reviews or testimonials. Share these snippets across your marketing channels to build credibility and encourage others to join in. People are more likely to purchase a product when they see others having a positive experience.

Realize that things might not go perfectly—and that's okay. Maybe your website crashes due to high traffic, or a social media ad doesn't perform as expected. Instead of panicking, have a contingency plan in place to address these issues quickly. A calm, solution-focused approach will help you navigate any obstacles that arise.

Furthermore, engage with your audience continually throughout the day. Respond to comments, answer questions, and thank customers for their support. The more interactive you are, the stronger the connection you'll

CHAPTER 14: LAUNCH DAY STRATEGY

build with your community. This engagement isn't just beneficial for launch day sales; it's an investment in long-term customer loyalty.

Utilize limited-time offers. People love deals, especially when they feel they're getting something exclusive. You can introduce flash sales, early bird specials, or bundle discounts. Not only do these offers create urgency, but they also increase the perceived value of your product. Ensure these deals are highlighted across all your marketing channels, so no one misses out.

Don't forget to analyze competitor behavior. Use tools to monitor their social media, websites, and marketing strategies. Observing their tactics can provide insights and reveal opportunities for differentiation. Maybe they missed a critical feature that you can emphasize, or perhaps their customer reviews highlight a common issue that your product solves. Use this information to your advantage.

Call in favors and leverage your network. This is where collaboration and partnerships can shine. Whether it's influencers, business partners, or satisfied customers, request them to spread the word about your launch. Having credible third parties vouch for your product can extend your reach considerably and build immediate trust.

Record the milestones and responses. Capture screenshots of social media interactions, high web traffic stats, and exceptional customer feedback. These moments not only serve as motivational reminders but can also be used for marketing materials in future campaigns. Documenting your journey provides material for a powerful story that resonates with potential customers down the line.

Stay fueled and hydrated. This might sound trivial, but launch day can be a marathon of its own. Keep snacks and water close by, and make sure to take short breaks. A well-nourished mind functions better, allowing you to think clearly and make sound decisions.

Finally, celebrate the small wins, even before the big results roll in. Whether it's your first sale, a highly positive review, or even just reaching a website visitor milestone—take a moment to acknowledge these achievements. Reward your team too; a happy team is a productive team.

Executing the perfect launch is more than just a culmination of efforts;

it's a dynamic exercise that can set the tone for your fledgling enterprise. This pivotal day warrants all your dedication, energy, and creativity. The groundwork you've laid has prepared you for this. Now, it's about showing the world what you have to offer. Go forth, execute flawlessly, and watch your dream take flight.

Chapter 15: Customer Acquisition

Now that you've got all the pieces in place for your business, it's time to dive into one of the most critical aspects: customer acquisition. This is where the magic happens and your efforts start to pay off. Begin by identifying key lead generation techniques tailored to your target audience—whether it's through social media, email marketing, or networking events, you need to find where your potential customers are and reach out to them persuasively. Use a combination of compelling content and irresistible offers to turn these leads into paying customers. Remember, the goal isn't just to get people to notice your business, but to guide them through a seamless journey from awareness to a purchase. In this phase, focus on building trust and rapport, helping you convert interest into sales, and laying a solid foundation for long-term customer relationships.

Lead Generation Techniques

Let's face it, without leads, your business is like a car without fuel—it simply won't go anywhere. Lead generation is the lifeline of customer acquisition, making it one of the most crucial elements to master when launching a million-dollar business in just 48 hours. This chapter will equip you with a variety of techniques to attract, engage, and convert prospects into paying customers.

First and foremost, understanding your ideal customer is key to effective lead generation. If you know who you're targeting, you can tailor your efforts to reach them more efficiently. Think of it as fishing with the right bait.

Whether you're targeting stay-at-home moms who value convenience or college students looking for budget-friendly options, your approach will differ. Customizing your message to resonate with your audience's particular needs and pain points is essential.

One of the quickest and most effective ways to generate leads is through social media. With billions of users across platforms like Facebook, Instagram, and LinkedIn, it's almost impossible not to find your target audience somewhere. Start by creating engaging content that offers value—think tutorials, quick tips, or even memes that relate to your business. Use paid ads to target specific demographics and interests, narrowing it down to those most likely to convert.

Email marketing remains a heavyweight champion in the lead generation arena. Building an email list from day one can be a goldmine for nurturing leads. Use opt-in forms on your website, social media pages, and even during offline events to capture email addresses. Offering incentives like discounts, free e-books, or exclusive content can entice people to join your list. Countless email marketing tools can automate the process, providing drip campaigns that keep your brand top-of-mind.

Search Engine Optimization (SEO) is another powerful tool at your disposal. Optimizing your website for search engines means you can attract organic traffic without spending a dime on ads. Make sure your website content is rich with the keywords your potential customers are searching for. Blog posts, product descriptions, and even image tags should be optimized to improve search rankings. This method might take a little time to yield results but investing in good SEO practices is worth it in the long run.

Networking events, although seemingly old-school, can be highly effective for lead generation. Local business meetups, industry conferences, or even online webinars can connect you with like-minded individuals and potential customers. Networking is not just about business cards and handshakes; it's about establishing authentic relationships. Don't underestimate the power of word-of-mouth referrals. Offering a compelling elevator pitch can make a lasting impression, but remember to listen just as much as you talk.

Webinars and live streams can position you as an authority in your field

CHAPTER 15: CUSTOMER ACQUISITION

while generating leads. Think about topics that could provide immense value to your target audience. Promote the event via your email list, social media channels, and even partnerships with influencers. During the event, make sure to collect attendees' contact information for follow-ups. Offering an exclusive deal or discount at the end of the webinar can encourage immediate action.

Content marketing is another valuable strategy. By creating high-quality blog posts, whitepapers, or e-books, you can attract people who are interested in what you have to offer. These pieces of content act as lead magnets, driving traffic to your website and encouraging visitors to hand over their contact information in exchange for valuable insights. The goal here is to provide content that solves a problem or answers a question your target audience has.

While we're on the topic of online strategies, don't overlook pay-per-click (PPC) advertising. Investing in PPC campaigns on Google Ads or Bing Ads can deliver almost instantaneous results. The key here is to use highly targeted keywords so you don't end up wasting money on irrelevant clicks. By directing users to a well-designed landing page optimized for conversions, you can turn those clicks into leads quickly.

Referral programs are a word-of-mouth lead generation technique on steroids. Encourage your existing customers to refer friends and family by offering them incentives. Maybe it's a discount on their next purchase, a free month of service, or a small gift card. Since people tend to trust recommendations from people they know, word-of-mouth referrals can be incredibly effective.

Let's not forget the power of partnerships and collaborations. Teaming up with complementary businesses can open doors to new customer bases. For instance, if you sell healthy snacks, partnering with a fitness blog for a joint giveaway could attract a highly-targeted audience. Cross-promotions can multiply your reach and credibility, making it easier and quicker to generate leads.

In the fast-paced world of business, speed matters. Utilize chatbots on your website to engage visitors instantly. Chatbots can answer questions, collect customer information, and guide users through your sales funnel in real time.

They can work 24/7, ensuring you never miss a potential lead even while you sleep.

Don't underestimate the effectiveness of contests and giveaways. People love free stuff, and they're often willing to provide their email address or engage with your brand on social media for a chance to win. This can dramatically increase your exposure and bring in a large number of leads quickly.

In summary, mastering lead generation involves a diversified approach. Relying on just one technique is seldom enough. Whether you're using social media, email marketing, SEO, networking, content marketing, PPC advertising, referral programs, partnerships, chatbots, or giveaways, each method has its unique advantages and can complement the others.

Equip yourself with these tools, adapt them to your specific audience, and watch as your leads multiply, setting the stage for substantial growth. Remember, the goal isn't just to generate leads but to turn them into loyal customers who believe in your brand as much as you do. The journey from lead generation to conversion may be intricate, but with the right techniques, it can be exceptionally rewarding.

Converting Leads to Customers

Congratulations, you've generated leads. Now, let's turn those leads into paying customers. This transformation is where all your preparation, marketing, and strategic efforts come to fruition. Converting leads into customers involves understanding their needs, nurturing relationships, and offering genuine solutions that resonate with them. It's an art and a science, and the quicker you master it, the faster you'll see success in your entrepreneurial journey.

First off, recognize that every lead represents a unique journey, a potential story of conversion. It's essential to fine-tune your communication to appeal directly to the interest and pain points of each lead. Through personalized emails, informative content, and timely interactions, you create an emotional connection that builds trust and persuades the lead to take the next step.

One critical aspect of successful conversion is to simplify the process. Make it as easy as possible for your leads to become customers. This means intuitive navigation on your website, clear calls to action, and easily accessible customer support. When potential customers don't face any friction, your conversion rates soar.

Automation tools can prove incredibly useful in this phase. Utilize email automation to send personalized follow-ups and reminders. Automated chatbots on your website can answer common questions and guide prospects toward a purchase. Remember, automation should enhance the personal touch, not replace it.

Remember that nurturing leads is not just about pushing for a sale. It's about providing value at every touchpoint. Share educational content, such as blog posts, webinars, or how-to guides that align with your product or service. This value-based approach not only positions you as an expert but also builds trust and rapport with your prospects.

Establishing a sense of urgency can significantly improve your conversion rates. Limited-time offers, exclusive deals, or countdown timers on your landing pages create a psychological trigger that compels leads to act quickly. However, ensure that any urgency you create is real and not just a sales gimmick.

Social proof and testimonials are another powerful tool in converting leads. Positive reviews and testimonials from existing customers can reassure potential buyers about the effectiveness and trustworthiness of your offerings. People are more likely to purchase when they see that others have had positive experiences.

Understanding and leveraging analytics is crucial. Use analytics tools to track how leads interact with your website and marketing campaigns. This data provides insights into what's working and what's not, allowing you to adjust your strategies accordingly. Conversion rates, bounce rates, and click-through rates are some of the key metrics you should closely monitor.

A seamless follow-up process is necessary. Often, leads need multiple interactions before they convert. Utilize a CRM (Customer Relationship Management) system to track and manage these interactions. Schedule regular follow-ups and ensure each communication offers value and encourages the lead to move further down the sales funnel.

Train your sales team well. They should understand the product inside out and be adept at handling objections. Role-playing different scenarios can be an effective way to prepare. Your salespeople should focus on listening more than selling, understanding the specific needs of each lead, and tailoring their pitch accordingly.

Creating a loyalty program even for new customers can be a strong pull. Offering a discount on their next purchase or a small freebie can incentivize the initial purchase. Once a lead has made a small commitment, they're more likely to become repeat customers. The initial conversion is just the beginning of a long-term relationship.

Also, refine your offer continually. Be open to feedback and willing to adapt. Sometimes slight adjustments in pricing, packaging, or delivery can have a significant impact on conversion rates. Always test and iterate your approach.

Lastly, maintain integrity throughout the process. Be honest about what your product or service can and cannot do. Misleading your leads may result in a quick sale, but it harms long-term trust and brand reputation. Authenticity fosters lasting customer relationships.

In conclusion, converting leads to customers is about building relationships, understanding needs, and providing value consistently. By employing a mix of strategic and tactical efforts, you'll see those leads turn into loyal, paying customers, driving your business forward. Keep learning, keep optimizing, and keep connecting with your audience authentically. The road to building a million-dollar business starts with mastering this critical step in your customer acquisition strategy.

Chapter 16: Scaling Your Operations

Now that you've got your business up and running, it's time to consider how to scale your operations without losing momentum or quality. Scaling doesn't just mean growing bigger; it means growing smarter. Streamlining processes is essential, so look at where automation can save time and reduce errors. This will free up your mental bandwidth to focus on creative problem-solving and strategic planning. Hiring the right people is equally critical, as you can't do everything yourself. The key is to identify tasks that can be outsourced or delegated. This not only helps to manage your workload but also brings in specialized expertise that can elevate your business to new heights. Remember, every hour you can redirect from routine tasks to strategic activities is an hour invested in the future growth of your business. As you bring new people into your team, make sure they share your vision and passion—culture fit can often be as important as skill set. So, take calculated risks and keep your eyes on the broader horizon. Your hustle today sets the foundation for a scalable, sustainable business tomorrow.

Streamlining Processes

Scaling your operations isn't just about doing more; it's about doing more efficiently. It's a crucial step that can make or break your business. Streamlining processes is the backbone of scaling, enabling you to handle increased demand without compromising on quality or customer satisfaction.

Let's start with a clear definition: streamlining processes means optimizing and simplifying the way tasks are accomplished within your business. This often involves eliminating unnecessary steps, improving communication, and utilizing technology to automate repetitive tasks.

One of the first areas to look at is your workflow. Break down every task from start to finish. Identify bottlenecks and redundant steps. Are there tasks that can be automated? For example, if you're spending too much time manually inputting data, investing in a simple software solution could save hours every week. It's all about making your workflow smoother and more efficient.

Consider your current communication channels. How streamlined are they? Effective communication is the bedrock of a well-oiled machine. Tools like Slack or Microsoft Teams can help centralize your communications, making it easier for everyone in your team to stay on the same page. Avoid missed messages and dropped tasks by having a clear protocol and using the right tools.

In documenting procedures, consistency is key. Create standard operating procedures (SOPs) for all recurring tasks. This ensures that everyone knows the best way to get things done. Whether it's onboarding a new employee or handling customer service inquiries, having an SOP means there's a tested and efficient method for everything. Plus, it makes it much easier to delegate tasks effectively.

Automation can be a game-changer. Today, there are myriad tools that can help automate different aspects of your business. From social media scheduling tools that post content automatically to customer relationship management (CRM) systems that track interactions and follow-ups with customers, automation helps you do more with less effort. Integrating these tools into your operations can significantly boost your productivity.

Inventory management is another aspect that can benefit greatly from streamlined processes. Proper inventory management ensures you always have what you need without overstocking. Employing inventory management software can help track stock levels, manage orders, and forecast demand, saving you from manual oversight and potential errors that could lead to stockouts or excess stock.

Finances can also be streamlined to save time and avoid errors. Automated accounting software can manage invoices, track expenses, and generate financial reports with minimal human intervention. These tools not only streamline your processes but also provide valuable insights into your financial health, aiding in more informed decision-making.

Customer service is an area where streamlining processes can have a direct impact on customer satisfaction and retention. Implementing a ticket system for handling support queries ensures all customer issues are tracked and resolved promptly. Chatbots can handle basic questions, freeing up your human staff to address more complex issues.

Remember, streamlining doesn't mean cutting corners. It's about working smarter, not harder. Lean into the power of technology to handle mundane tasks so you can focus on driving growth and innovation. Regularly review your processes and seek feedback from your team. They're often aware of inefficiencies and have insights into how things can be improved.

Time management tools can also play a significant role in streamlining. Tools like Asana or Trello help you prioritize tasks and keep track of deadlines, ensuring that your team stays productive. These platforms enable you to assign tasks, set deadlines, and monitor progress without endless email chains or meetings.

While at it, don't underestimate the power of delegation and outsourcing. As your business grows, you'll find that you can't do everything yourself. Delegating tasks to your team or outsourcing functions like marketing or accounting can free up your time to focus on strategic decisions. It's about leveraging other people's expertise to keep all parts of your business running smoothly.

Finally, measure and analyze. Use KPIs (Key Performance Indicators) to track performance and identify areas for improvement. Whether it's turnaround time, cost per acquisition, or order fulfillment accuracy, having solid metrics ensures you're making data-driven decisions. Regularly review these metrics and tweak processes accordingly.

Streamlining processes is not a one-time task but an ongoing effort. Always be on the lookout for new tools, technologies, and methods that can make your business more efficient. Engage with your team, gather their insights, and be open to change. Efficiency is the foundation of scalability, enabling you to handle growth sustainably and profitably.

Hiring and Outsourcing

When you're on the fast track to scaling your operations, the concept of hiring and outsourcing becomes indispensable. Building a million-dollar business in 48 hours isn't just about having a great idea and a solid plan; it's about leveraging the right talent and resources to execute that plan efficiently.

Think of hiring and outsourcing as strategic chess moves. You're not just looking to fill gaps; you're aiming to position experts where they can make the most significant impact. The goal is to stay lean while maximizing productivity. Even in the first 48 hours, identifying key roles that need immediate attention can set the stage for success.

Most entrepreneurs at this stage are driven by the 'do-it-yourself' mentality. While this attitude is commendable, it can also be a pitfall. Delegation is a skill that must be learned if you want to scale quickly. Recognizing that you can't do everything yourself is the first step toward sustainable growth. Identify tasks that are outside your core competencies and outsource them to professionals.

Start by listing out all the tasks required to launch and scale your business. These tasks will fall into various categories such as administrative work, customer service, marketing, and product development. Evaluate which tasks you can delegate immediately and find qualified professionals to handle them. A virtual assistant, for example, can handle administrative tasks, freeing up your time to focus on strategy and growth.

Many successful entrepreneurs emphasize the importance of hiring smartly. It's not just about finding someone who can do the job; it's about finding someone who fits well with your company culture and understands your vision. Take the time to conduct thorough interviews, even if it's virtual. Ask questions that dig into their problem-solving abilities, their experience in similar roles, and their understanding of your industry.

CHAPTER 16: SCALING YOUR OPERATIONS

When it comes to outsourcing, platforms like Upwork, Fiverr, and Toptal can be invaluable. These platforms give you access to a global talent pool, allowing you to find specialists who can complete tasks ranging from graphic design to software development. Be precise in your job postings and include specific requirements and expectations. Clear communication is crucial to get the most out of your outsourcing efforts.

One of the key advantages of outsourcing is flexibility. Unlike full-time employees, outsourced workers can be hired on a project basis. This flexibility is vital when you're attempting to scale quickly. You don't want to be bogged down by lengthy HR processes. Having the ability to bring in experts as and when needed allows you to stay nimble and react to market demands more efficiently.

Cost is another factor to consider. While hiring full-time employees incurs additional expenses like benefits and office space, outsourcing tends to be more cost-effective. You pay only for the services you need, when you need them. This model is particularly beneficial for startups operating on a tight budget. However, always ensure that you vet the service providers thoroughly to avoid any unforeseen costs due to subpar work.

Negotiate contracts that are clear and concise. Outline the scope of work, timelines, and payment terms in detail. This minimizes the risk of misunderstandings and ensures that everyone is on the same page. A well-drafted contract not only protects your interests but also sets the stage for a successful working relationship.

To maintain quality control, establish a robust feedback mechanism. Regular check-ins and updates allow you to monitor progress and make adjustments as needed. Don't hesitate to provide constructive feedback and ask for revisions when necessary. The more closely you can track the performance of your hired talent, the easier it will be to ensure that they're meeting your business goals.

In cases where the work quality is consistently outstanding, consider long-term arrangements. Having a go-to person or team for specific tasks can drastically reduce the time spent on onboarding and training new contractors. Building a reliable network of freelancers can offer the best of both worlds:

flexibility and consistency.

Another strategic approach is hiring part-time employees or interns. This can be a cost-effective way to bring in fresh talent, especially for roles that require less specialization but are still critical to daily operations. Onboarding part-time employees allows you to test the waters before committing to a full-time hire.

Invest in training and development for your team and contractors. Training ensures that everyone is aligned with your business objectives and understands your expectations. The better equipped your team is, the more efficient they will be. This investment in professional development will pay off in the long run through increased productivity and quality of work.

Embracing technology can further streamline the hiring and outsourcing process. Tools like Slack for communication, Trello for project management, and Google Workspace for collaboration can make working with remote teams seamless. Automation tools can handle repetitive tasks, allowing your team to focus on more strategic initiatives.

Culture plays a crucial role in the success of your hiring and outsourcing strategy. Even if you're working with remote teams or freelancers, fostering a positive work culture can lead to higher levels of engagement and productivity. Celebrate achievements, encourage open communication, and make everyone feel like they are a part of the mission.

Finally, remember that scaling your operations involves continuous learning and adaptation. The first hires and outsourcing partnerships you establish may not be perfect, and that's okay. Learn from each experience, refine your approach, and keep looking for ways to improve. Your ability to build and manage a talented and effective team will be a cornerstone of your success.

In conclusion, hiring and outsourcing are not just operational tasks; they are strategic moves that can accelerate your growth. Leveraging the right talent and resources allows you to focus on what you do best, driving your business towards that million-dollar mark. So, think critically, act wisely, and watch your business flourish.

Chapter 17: Financial Management

Managing your business's finances effectively is crucial for long-term success, and it starts with mastering budgeting and forecasting. A well-crafted budget acts as your financial roadmap, helping you allocate resources efficiently and prioritize spending. Meanwhile, accurate forecasting allows you to anticipate future revenues and costs, enabling you to make informed decisions quickly. Remember to take tax considerations into account; understanding your taxation obligations can save you from costly penalties and keep your business compliant. By ensuring robust financial management, you're laying a solid foundation that will support your startup's growth and sustainability. This dual approach not only secures your current operations but also arms you with the financial insight needed to seize new opportunities and tackle challenges head-on.

Budgeting and Forecasting

If you're on the brink of launching your million-dollar business, the importance of budgeting and forecasting simply can't be overstated. These aren't just financial exercises; they're the backbone of your strategic planning. Budgeting ensures that you allocate your resources efficiently, while forecasting helps you predict future financial conditions, allowing you to make informed decisions. Think of these tools as the GPS for your entrepreneurial journey—they guide you toward your financial goals, adjusting for detours along the way.

It's crucial to understand that a budget is more than just a spreadsheet filled with numbers. At its core, a budget is a financial plan for allocating resources based on your business goals. Start by outlining all expected income and expenses. Income could come from sales, investments, or any other revenue streams you plan to tap into. Expenses, on the other hand, will include everything—rent, utilities, materials, labor, marketing costs, and even those pesky little expenses that often go overlooked.

Don't overlook seasonal fluctuations in income and expenses either. For instance, if you're selling holiday-specific products, you'll likely see a spike in revenue during certain months. Similarly, some expenses, like heating in winter, may not be consistent throughout the year. Anticipate these fluctuations to keep your budget realistic and adaptable.

Now, let's talk forecasting. Forecasting isn't just looking into a crystal ball; it's data-driven prediction based on historical performance, market trends, and key indicators. Start simple: use tools like Excel or Google Sheets to track your revenue and expenses over several months. As you gather more data, you'll get better at predicting future trends. Accurate forecasting can help you avoid cash crunches, make informed investment decisions, and adjust your strategy on the fly.

For the novice entrepreneur, budget and forecasting might sound intimidating. However, think of them as an ongoing process rather than a one-time task. Begin with broad estimates and refine them as your business grows and you gather more data. Don't be afraid to revise your forecasts frequently; they're not set in stone. Adaptability is key.

To give you more confidence, here are some practical tips for effective budgeting and forecasting:

- **Leverage Software Tools:** From QuickBooks to Xero, there are numerous tools designed to simplify the budgeting and forecasting process. These tools can automate data entry, generate reports, and even offer valuable insights based on your data.
- **Separate Personal and Business Finances:** Keeping your finances separate is crucial for accurate budgeting. Open a separate bank account solely for your business. This will make tracking income and expenses

far easier.
- **Update Regularly:** Your budget and forecasts should be living documents. Update them monthly or quarterly to reflect actual performance and account for any changes or unforeseen costs.
- **Scenario Planning:** Always prepare for multiple scenarios—best case, worst case, and most likely. This helps in planning for opportunities and mitigating risks.
- **Consult Experts if Needed:** If numbers aren't your forte, consider hiring a financial advisor or accountant, even if it's just for a one-time consultation to get you started on the right foot.

Another vital aspect is cash flow management. While budgeting helps you plan, managing your cash flow ensures you have enough liquidity to meet your obligations. Always keep an eye on your cash inflows and outflows to avoid any hiccups. For instance, if most of your revenue is coming from invoices that are due in 30 or 60 days, but your expenses are immediate, you could run into trouble. Consider options like invoice factoring or short-term loans to bridge these gaps.

Furthermore, link your budgeting and forecasting to your business goals. For example, if your goal is to expand your product line, you'll need to allocate budget toward product development, marketing, and perhaps additional labor. Your forecasts should then reflect an increase in revenue and expenses associated with this expansion. It's a dynamic cycle: goals inform your budget, and your financial reality informs your goals.

In addition, keep an eye on key performance indicators (KPIs) relevant to your business. These might include conversion rates, customer acquisition costs, and return on investment (ROI) for marketing campaigns. Tracking these KPIs allows you to adjust your budget and forecasts based on actual performance, providing a more accurate roadmap for achieving your goals.

Remember, entrepreneurship is as much about managing risks as it is about seizing opportunities. Effective budgeting and forecasting equip you to do both. Don't be disheartened by initial bumps; they're part and parcel of the entrepreneurial journey. Each budgeting cycle will provide you with valuable insights and lessons, making your forecasts more accurate and your plans more robust.

Ultimately, your willingness to dive into the "numbers game" will set the stage for your business's financial success. A well-thought-out budget, complemented by accurate forecasting, will not only keep you financially healthy but will also actively drive your business toward its million-dollar goal. So roll up your sleeves, put in the effort, and keep your eyes on the prize. The fusion of vision and financial discipline is the formula that turns a weekend hustle into a thriving, scalable enterprise.

Tax Considerations

Understanding tax considerations is an essential aspect of financial management for any side hustler, business owner, or entrepreneur. With the right knowledge and strategies, you can navigate the complexities of the tax system to maximize your earnings and ensure compliance. Taxes may not be the most glamorous part of running a business, but they play a crucial role in ensuring your venture's long-term success and stability.

First, let's talk about different business structures and how they affect your tax responsibilities. Whether you're a sole proprietor, part of a partnership, or have established a limited liability company (LLC), each structure comes with unique tax implications. It's vital to choose the right one for your business model to optimize your tax situation. For instance, a sole proprietorship is straightforward and easy to manage, with income reported on your personal tax return. However, it exposes you to personal liability for business debts and obligations.

An LLC, on the other hand, offers more protection by separating your personal assets from your business liabilities. It also provides flexibility in how you choose to be taxed, either as a sole proprietorship, partnership, or corporation. Understanding these distinctions is the first step in managing your tax responsibilities efficiently. Consulting with an accountant or tax advisor can provide invaluable insights tailored to your business needs.

Next, let's dive into the importance of keeping detailed records. Accurate record-keeping is not just about being organized; it's a legal requirement. You need to keep track of all income and expenses related to your business activities. This includes receipts, invoices, bank statements, and payroll records. Good record-keeping makes it easier to prepare your tax returns, claim deductions, and provide documentation in case of an audit.

One of the biggest advantages of having a side hustle or running a small business is the ability to deduct business expenses. From vehicle use and home office space to marketing and professional services, there are many deductions available to reduce your taxable income. However, it's essential to differentiate between personal and business expenses. The IRS has strict rules about what qualifies as a deductible expense, so make sure you stay compliant to avoid penalties.

Estimated tax payments are another crucial aspect of tax considerations. Unlike traditional employees who have taxes withheld from their paychecks, business owners and freelancers must make quarterly estimated tax payments. This means you need to calculate and pay your taxes every quarter based on your expected annual income. Failure to do so can result in hefty penalties and interest charges. Tools and resources like accounting software can simplify this process by helping you calculate and track your tax obligations.

Sales tax is another area that can be a bit of a minefield, especially if you're selling products or services in multiple states or online. Sales tax regulations vary significantly from state to state, and keeping up with these changes can be challenging. The key is to know where your business has a tax nexus, meaning a significant presence requiring you to collect and remit sales taxes. Some states also have specific registration and reporting requirements, so make sure you understand your obligations to avoid fines.

International sales introduce an additional layer of complexity to your tax considerations. Different countries have varying tax laws, and you may be required to pay value-added tax (VAT) or goods and services tax (GST) on international sales. Understanding the tax treaties and agreements between countries can help minimize double taxation and ensure compliance with international tax laws. International tax specialists can provide guidance in navigating these complexities.

One of the best practices in managing your taxes is to separate your personal and business finances. Opening a dedicated business bank account and using a business credit card can help you track your business expenses more effectively. This will also make it easier to provide accurate financial statements and tax returns, reducing the risk of errors and potential audits.

Let's not forget about self-employment taxes, which consist of Social Security and Medicare taxes. If you're self-employed, you're responsible for both the employer and employee portions of these taxes. However, you can deduct half of your self-employment tax when calculating your adjusted gross income, which can reduce your overall tax liability. Making timely estimated tax payments can help you manage these obligations and avoid surprises when your tax returns are due.

Tax credits are often overlooked but can provide significant tax savings. Unlike deductions, which reduce your taxable income, tax credits reduce your tax liability dollar-for-dollar. Examples of business tax credits include the Small Business Health Care Tax Credit, which helps small businesses provide health insurance to employees, and the Research and Development Tax Credit, which encourages innovation and technological advancement. Staying informed about available tax credits can result in substantial savings for your business.

Tax planning isn't just a year-end activity; it's an ongoing process that requires regular review and adjustment. Setting aside time every month or quarter to review your financial statements, assess your tax liabilities, and adjust your strategies can help you stay ahead of your tax obligations. Planning ahead for potential tax reforms and changes in tax laws can also help you adapt your business strategies and minimize your tax burden.

Finally, don't underestimate the value of professional help. Tax laws are complex and ever-changing, and the consequences of getting it wrong can be severe. Hiring a qualified accountant or tax advisor can provide peace of mind and allow you to focus on growing your business. Professionals can help you navigate the intricacies of tax regulations, identify applicable deductions and credits, and ensure compliance with all legal requirements.

Tax considerations may seem daunting, but with careful planning, sound record-keeping, and professional guidance, you can manage them effectively. By staying informed and proactive, you can ensure that taxes don't become a stumbling block on your path to building a million-dollar business. Instead, they can be a well-managed aspect of your financial strategy, allowing you to focus on what you do best: innovating, growing, and succeeding.

Remember, taxes are a part of the business landscape. Learning to navigate this terrain successfully is a skill that can set you apart as a savvy entrepreneur. So take the time to understand your tax obligations, leverage available resources, and seek professional advice when needed. Doing so will put you on a solid foundation for financial management and long-term success.

Chapter 18: Customer Retention

Customer retention is not just a strategy; it's an art that can turn your fledgling endeavor into a thriving business. Focus on creating exceptional customer experiences that exceed expectations from the moment of first contact. Consider implementing loyalty programs that reward repeat business, making customers feel valued and appreciated. Excellent customer service is key—prompt responses, resolving issues efficiently, and going the extra mile can transform one-time buyers into lifelong advocates. Remember, it's far more cost-effective to keep an existing customer happy than to acquire a new one. Plus, satisfied customers often become your most powerful marketing tool through word-of-mouth referrals and positive reviews. By making customer satisfaction a cornerstone of your business, you're setting the stage for sustainable growth and long-term success.

Building Loyalty Programs

When aiming to transform a side hustle into a million-dollar business, customer retention is crucial. One of the most effective ways to achieve this is by building loyalty programs. These programs go beyond just offering discounts; they create a connection that keeps customers coming back, fostering sustainable growth. Let's dissect how you can craft a compelling loyalty program that serves both your business and your customer base.

First and foremost, understand the magic of personalization. Consumers today expect businesses to understand them almost intuitively. Use data to offer rewards that resonate. For instance, if you run a subscription box service, recognizing loyal customers with a tailor-made box based on their previous purchases can make a significant impact. The goal here is to create the feeling that they're getting something special, just for them.

One key element is simplicity. Your loyalty program should be easy to understand and use. Overcomplicating the requirements or the reward structure will only frustrate customers. The easier it is for them to see the benefits, the more likely they are to participate. Think of Starbucks' Rewards program: points accumulate quickly, and customers can easily track and redeem them using the app or in-store.

Introduce tiers to your program. Tiers add a gamification element to your loyalty scheme, encouraging customers to spend more to reach higher levels for better rewards. For example, you could have Bronze, Silver, and Gold tiers, each offering greater benefits. Just be sure to clearly communicate how customers can advance through these tiers and what they'll gain at each level.

Feedback is another cornerstone. Use your loyalty program as a channel to solicit customer opinions. By involving them in the development of new products or the refinement of services, you enhance their emotional investment in your brand. Send out surveys or host community forums where members can share their thoughts. This not only makes customers feel valued but also provides invaluable insights into how you can improve.

Incentivize social sharing. When customers share their purchases or experiences on social media, they're doing free advertising for you. Offer points or rewards for social actions like sharing a post about your product, tagging your brand, or writing a review. This expands your reach considerably and shows potential customers that others are enthusiastic about what you're offering.

Technology can be your best ally. Utilize CRM (Customer Relationship Management) systems to track customer behavior and tailor rewards accordingly. If a customer habitually purchases a particular type of product, offer them discounts or exclusive access to similar items. This makes the customer feel understood and valued, increasing the likelihood of repeat business.

Events and exclusivity can also play a significant role. Hosting exclusive events or sales for loyalty program members makes them feel like they're part of an inner circle. This could be virtual events like webinars and Q&A sessions or physical events such as launch parties and pop-up shops. Such initiatives foster a community feeling among your customers, making them more likely to stay loyal.

Transparency is crucial. Customers need to trust that the loyalty program is fair and that their efforts to gain rewards will pay off. Regularly update them on their status and progress through emails or app notifications. Transparency builds trust, which is integral to any customer retention strategy.

Don't forget the power of surprise. Introducing surprise rewards or "just because" gifts can delight customers and keep them engaged. It doesn't have to be extravagant; even a small token can convey appreciation and make a customer feel special. Such unexpected bonuses can reignite interest in your brand and incentivize further purchases.

Finally, integrate your loyalty program seamlessly across all platforms. Whether customers are interacting with you online, via a mobile app, or in a physical store, their loyalty benefits should be easily accessible. Consistency in their experience ensures that they don't abandon the program out of frustration over technical glitches or discrepancies.

In conclusion, a thoughtfully constructed loyalty program can serve as a powerful tool in your customer retention arsenal. By focusing on personalization, simplicity, tier-based rewards, feedback incorporation, social sharing incentives, technological integration, exclusive events, transparency, surprise rewards, and seamless integration, you can create a program that not only retains customers but also turns them into avid brand advocates. This, in turn, drives sustainable growth and helps transform your business ambitions into reality.

CHAPTER 18: CUSTOMER RETENTION

Creating Exceptional Customer Service

When it comes to customer retention, creating exceptional customer service is non-negotiable. It's the glue that holds your business together and makes customers come back for more. Think of it as the foundation upon which all other business strategies rest. In today's hyper-competitive market, a stellar product or service alone isn't enough. Customers remember—and often cherish—how you made them feel. A remarkable customer service experience can turn a first-time buyer into a loyal advocate for your brand.

One of the simplest, yet most effective, ways to offer exceptional customer service is by being genuinely responsive and accessible. Whether it's through emails, phone calls, or social media messages, prompt and thoughtful responses make all the difference. Prioritize your customer's needs by replying within an acceptable timeframe—preferably within 24 hours. Quick responses show that you value their time and concerns, which fosters trust and loyalty. It's impressive how much goodwill you can generate just by paying attention and acting promptly.

Another way to elevate your customer service is by personalizing the experience. Know your customers by name, understand their preferences, and remember their past interactions with your business. When you demonstrate that you know and appreciate their unique needs, they'll feel valued rather than just another transaction. For example, if you're operating a boutique, keeping a record of customers' past purchases can allow you to recommend new products that are in line with their tastes. Personal touches like these build stronger, emotional connections between your business and your customers.

Effective communication is also key. Be clear, concise, and honest. If a product is delayed or there is an issue, inform your customer right away and explain the steps you're taking to resolve it. Transparency cultivates trust. Customers appreciate knowing what to expect and are generally more forgiving when issues are communicated proactively. Think about it—no one likes being kept in the dark. Keeping your customers informed can turn potentially negative situations into opportunities for demonstrating reliability and integrity.

Training your team to deliver superior customer service is another crucial component. This isn't a one-time endeavor but an ongoing commitment. Regular training sessions help ensure your team is well-equipped to handle any customer situation with grace and professionalism. Encourage them to go above and beyond, whether it's by offering a warm greeting, actively listening to concerns, or providing thoughtful solutions. Workshops and role-playing exercises can be especially effective in aligning your team with your customer service vision.

Empower your employees to make decisions. When your team feels they have the autonomy to solve problems on the spot, it leads to quicker resolutions and happier customers. There's nothing more frustrating for a customer than being bounced from one person to the next. Empowered employees can address issues more efficiently and effectively, which results in higher customer satisfaction rates and increased loyalty.

Technology can also play a significant role in enhancing your customer service. Utilize customer relationship management (CRM) software to keep track of customer interactions and preferences. Automated responses can manage frequently asked questions and common inquiries, freeing up your team to handle more complex issues. However, be careful not to overly rely on automation. There's a balance to be struck between using technology to streamline processes and maintaining the human touch that customers crave.

Never underestimate the power of feedback. Regularly solicit feedback from your customers through surveys, reviews, or direct conversations. Not only does this show customers that you value their opinions, but it also provides invaluable insights into areas where you can improve. Act on this feedback and be sure to communicate back any changes or improvements you've made as a result. This creates a feedback loop that continually enhances your customer service.

Moreover, create an environment of consistency. Customers should know that no matter who they talk to or when they contact you, they will receive the same high level of service. Standardize your service protocols and workflows to ensure consistency across all touchpoints. Whether someone shops online or walks into a physical store, their experience should feel seamless and uniform.

Incentivizing your customer service team can also lead to exceptional outcomes. Recognize and reward team members who consistently deliver outstanding service. This could be in the form of bonuses, public recognition, or even promotions. When your team feels appreciated and motivated, they're more likely to go the extra mile for your customers. A happy, motivated team often results in happy, loyal customers.

Another valuable tactic is implementing a follow-up strategy. After resolving an issue or completing a transaction, reach out to the customer to ensure they're satisfied with their experience. This additional touchpoint can resolve lingering issues and demonstrates that you care about their overall satisfaction. A simple follow-up email or a quick phone call can make a lasting impression and solidify customer loyalty.

Let's not forget the importance of creating a positive emotional experience. Emotion plays a huge role in customer satisfaction and loyalty. Small gestures like a handwritten thank you note, a surprise discount, or even remembering a customer's birthday can evoke positive emotions and make them feel special. Happy customers are not just more likely to return; they are also more likely to refer your business to others.

Your environment can also contribute to exceptional customer service. A clean, well-organized, and inviting space—whether it's a physical store or an online platform—creates a pleasant experience for your customers. Pay attention to the details, from the ease of navigation on your website to the ambiance of your store. Every element should work together to create a welcoming atmosphere that enhances the customer's overall experience.

Lastly, always be willing to go the extra mile. Sometimes it's the little things, like staying open a bit later for a last-minute shopper or offering an unexpected freebie, that leave the biggest impression. Customers remember businesses that made them feel special and valued. These moments build not just customer satisfaction but real loyalty and a sense of community around your brand.

Exceptional customer service is not an overnight project—it's an ongoing commitment to putting your customers first. It's about creating memorable experiences, solving problems efficiently, and continually finding ways to exceed expectations. The return on investment is incalculable, but one thing is certain: customers who feel cared for will keep coming back, bringing along friends and spreading the word. That kind of loyalty is priceless and a crucial ingredient for building a million-dollar business in just 48 hours.

Chapter 19: Leveraging Technology

In today's fast-paced world, capitalizing on technology is not just an option; it's a necessity for anyone aiming to launch a million-dollar business over a weekend. From essential tools and software to automation systems that streamline your operations, technology can significantly boost your efficiency and scalability. Embracing the right tech solutions allows you to automate mundane tasks, manage customer relationships, and optimize marketing efforts with precision. Think of technology as a force multiplier; by integrating suitable platforms and applications, you can focus more on strategic decisions and less on operational hurdles. With the multitude of cost-effective tools available, even side hustlers and stay-at-home parents can level the playing field and compete with larger enterprises. The key is to select technology that aligns with your business goals and enhances your ability to deliver value swiftly and effectively.

Essential Tools and Software

Leveraging technology is critical to transforming your business idea into a million-dollar venture, especially when working under tight timelines like 48 hours. In today's fast-paced digital era, the right tools and software can not only streamline your operations but also amplify your reach, allowing you to get more done in less time. Whether you're a business owner, a student juggling multiple responsibilities, or a stay-at-home parent looking to turn a side hustle into a full-time business, the tools you choose can make all the difference. In this section, we'll cover some of the essential technologies that can help you hit the ground running.

First and foremost, productivity and project management tools are non-negotiable. Tools like **Trello** and **Asana** offer intuitive interfaces for managing tasks, setting deadlines, and collaborating with team members. These platforms allow you to break down your project into manageable chunks, making it easier to stick to your 48-hour timeline. *Imagine being able to see every component of your business plan laid out in a clear, visual format; it's like having a road map that keeps you on track.*

Next, let's talk about communication. Seamless communication is vital for the success of any business. **Slack** is a popular tool that facilitates real-time communication and collaboration. It integrates with numerous other platforms, making it easier to centralize your operations. *Whether you're coordinating with a team or just organizing your thoughts, Slack's channels and direct messaging features ensure that nothing falls through the cracks.*

For document creation and file sharing, **Google Workspace** is indispensable. From Google Docs for word processing to Google Sheets for spreadsheets, you'll find everything you need to draft business plans, create marketing materials, and track your progress. The real-time collaboration features are particularly beneficial; multiple users can work on a document simultaneously, speeding up the brainstorming and decision-making process.

Of course, having a robust online presence is crucial. **Website builders** like *Wix* and *Squarespace* offer user-friendly platforms for creating professional-looking websites without needing any coding skills. In just a few hours, you can have a fully-functional website that serves as your business's digital storefront. For those who want more control and customization, *WordPress* is another excellent option, though it may require a steeper learning curve.

Social media management is another area where the right tools can save you a ton of time. **Hootsuite** and **Buffer** allow you to schedule posts across multiple social media platforms, track engagement, and analyze performance. This means you can focus more energy on creating valuable content and less on the manual, repetitive tasks of posting and monitoring. *Engaging with your audience consistently can significantly boost your brand's visibility and credibility,* *and these tools make it easier to achieve that.*

E-commerce platforms are also essential if you're selling products or services online. **Shopify** is a go-to platform for many entrepreneurs, given its ease of use and extensive features, including payment gateways, inventory management, and customer relationship management. *Setting up an online store on Shopify can be done in a matter of hours, and its built-in tools provide everything you need to start selling immediately.* If you're looking for alternatives, *WooCommerce* (a WordPress plugin) and *BigCommerce* are also worth exploring.

In terms of financial management, having a reliable accounting software is a must. Solutions like **QuickBooks** and **FreshBooks** simplify the process of tracking expenses, sending invoices, and managing cash flow. These tools can sync with your bank accounts, providing real-time updates on your financial status. *By keeping your finances organized and transparent, you can make better business decisions and avoid costly mistakes.*

*If you're into email marketing, platforms like **Mailchimp** and **ConvertKit** can help you build and manage your email lists, design marketing campaigns, and track their performance.* A well-executed email marketing campaign can be one of the most effective ways to convert leads into customers, and these platforms offer a plethora of templates and automation tools to streamline the process.

Moreover, graphic design and content creation tools can help you create compelling visuals and marketing materials. **Canva** is a user-friendly option for designing everything from social media posts to business cards. Its drag-and-drop interface and extensive template library make it accessible even for those with no design experience. For more advanced needs, Adobe's **Creative Cloud** suite offers industry-standard tools like Photoshop and Illustrator.

Customer relationship management (CRM) tools are vital for keeping track of your customer interactions and improving your service. Platforms like **HubSpot** and **Salesforce** offer comprehensive solutions for managing customer data, tracking sales pipelines, and automating marketing tasks. *These tools ensure that you never miss a follow-up and that every customer interaction is logged, helping you build stronger, more personal relationships* with your clients.

Data analytics tools like **Google Analytics** and **Mixpanel** are invaluable for understanding your audience and optimizing your business strategies. These tools provide insights into user behavior, traffic sources, and conversion rates, allowing you to make data-driven decisions. *By regularly analyzing this data, you can fine-tune your marketing efforts and improve your website's performance, leading to increased sales and customer satisfaction.*

For those interested in automating repetitive tasks, **Zapier** is a game-changer. It allows you to create "zaps" that automate workflows between different apps and services. For example, you can set up a zap to automatically add new email subscribers to your CRM or post new blog entries to your social media accounts. *The time saved by automating these small, yet important tasks can be better spent on higher-value activities that grow your business.*

Security is another critical area that should not be overlooked. Using password managers like **LastPass** or **Dashlane** can help you manage and secure your passwords more efficiently. Additionally, implementing two-factor authentication (2FA) and using VPN services can add extra layers of security, protecting your business from cyber threats.

Finally, don't forget about backups. Tools like **Dropbox** *and* **Google Drive** *offer cloud storage solutions that automatically back up your important files.* These services ensure that you have access to your documents anytime, anywhere, and can recover them in case of accidental deletion or hardware failure.

In summary, leveraging the right tools and software can significantly enhance your productivity

Automation and Efficiency

Time is one of your most valuable resources, and leveraging automation can help you make the most of it. For someone who is starting a business in under 48 hours, automating repetitive tasks frees up time for high-impact activities. Think of automation as your silent business partner, working round the clock to handle mundane tasks so you don't have to.

One of the first areas where automation can make a significant impact is in customer communications. From the moment a potential customer interacts with your business, be it through your website or social media, you can set up automated responses to guide them through their journey. Email marketing platforms like Mailchimp or ConvertKit allow you to create automated email sequences. This means that once a user subscribes, they can receive a welcome email followed by a series of targeted messages that introduce your products and services, all without you lifting a finger.

In addition to email automation, customer relationship management (CRM) systems like HubSpot or Salesforce can keep track of customer interactions, schedule follow-ups, and even automate some sales tasks. The beauty of CRM systems is that they centralize all your customer data, making it easier to manage relationships and streamline sales processes. With automated reminders and task assignments, your team can follow up on leads promptly, enhancing customer retention and satisfaction.

Social media is another critical area where automation can save time and increase efficiency. Tools like Hootsuite, Buffer, and Later allow you to schedule posts across multiple platforms well in advance. This ensures consistent engagement with your audience without the need for you to be online 24/7. Additionally, you can use chatbots on platforms like Facebook Messenger to handle customer inquiries. These bots can answer frequently asked questions, provide product information, and even process orders, all while you focus on growing your business.

Consider leveraging e-commerce automation tools if your business involves online sales. Platforms like Shopify, WooCommerce, and BigCommerce offer various plugins to automate tasks such as inventory management, order processing, and even customer follow-ups. Imagine the relief of knowing that the moment a customer makes a purchase, your system automatically updates inventory levels, processes the payment, and sends out confirmation emails—all without manual intervention.

bookkeeping and accounting are other areas ripe for automation. Software solutions such as QuickBooks, Xero, and FreshBooks can automate invoicing, payroll, and expense tracking. Automated financial reports and analytics can give critical insights into your business's health, helping you make more informed decisions.

Moreover, look into using Project Management tools like Asana, Trello, or Monday.com to streamline your workflow and manage tasks more effectively. These platforms allow you to set up tasks, assign them to team members, and track progress—providing a clear overview of your business activities and deadlines. They often offer automation features that can, for instance, automatically move a task to the next stage once it's completed, notify team members of updates, or even generate reports on project status.

Marketing automation is another game-changer for busy entrepreneurs. Tools like HubSpot, Marketo, and ActiveCampaign help you streamline your marketing campaigns. You can set up workflows that trigger specific actions based on customer behaviors. For instance, a customer who abandons their shopping cart might receive an automated follow-up email with a discount offer to encourage them to complete their purchase.

Data analytics can also be automated to provide you with valuable insights without manual effort. Google Analytics, for instance, can automatically send you customized reports summarizing website activity. This helps you quickly identify trends, track the success of marketing campaigns, and make data-driven decisions.

It's easy to see how automation and efficiency can play a crucial role in scaling your operations. As your business grows, the volume of tasks can become overwhelming, making automation even more critical. By integrating automation early, you lay a foundation for scalable growth that doesn't compromise on quality or customer satisfaction.

Another area where automation shines is in customer service. Tools like Zendesk and Intercom offer automated ticketing systems that prioritize and categorize customer inquiries. These tools can also send automated acknowledgment emails, reassuring customers that their concerns are being addressed. This not only improves response times but also ensures no customer query falls through the cracks.

Don't forget about content creation and curation. Tools like Canva and Buffer's Pablo can help you automate parts of your content creation process. Canva's templates allow you to quickly create professional-quality graphics, while Pablo by Buffer offers an easy way to create images tailored for social media sharing. Although creativity can't be fully automated, these tools can significantly cut down the time spent on these tasks.

Finally, personal productivity tools like IFTTT (If This Then That) and Zapier can help automate routine activities that may not fit into conventional categories. For instance, you can use these tools to automate everything from saving email attachments to a specific Dropbox folder, to setting up complex workflows that integrate multiple apps. The possibilities are endless and can be tailored to your unique business needs.

Of course, while automating tasks and processes can save time and reduce errors, it's important to regularly review and optimize these systems. Automation should enhance your business operations, not complicate them. Periodically evaluate the performance of your automated systems to ensure they are functioning as intended and making the desired impact.

Embracing automation and striving for efficiency doesn't mean that every aspect of your business should be robotic. There's enormous value in human touch, particularly in customer interactions and creative processes. The goal is to automate those repetitive and time-consuming tasks so that you and your team can focus on areas where human ingenuity and personal connection make the most difference.

In summary, leveraging automation and focusing on efficiency are essential strategies for anyone looking to build a successful business in a short period. By smartly integrating automation tools into your workflow, you'll free up valuable time that can be better spent on strategic planning, innovation, and personal growth—key components in your journey to creating a million-dollar business in just 48 hours. Embrace these tools, optimize your processes, and watch as your productivity soars, bringing your entrepreneurial dreams ever closer to reality.

Chapter 20: Building a Strong Team

As you embark on your journey to build a million-dollar business in 48 hours, assembling a strong team is indispensable. Your team's talent, cohesion, and shared vision can significantly elevate your business trajectory, making or breaking your venture. Look for individuals whose skills complement your own and who are as passionate about the project's success as you are. Leadership in this context isn't just about delegating tasks; it is about fostering an environment where creativity and mutual respect thrive. Establish clear roles and open channels of communication, ensuring everyone is aligned with the mission and objectives. Remember, a well-rounded team amplifies your capabilities, turning ambitious ideas into executable plans swiftly and efficiently.

Recruiting Talent

As you venture into the world of entrepreneurship, one of the most crucial steps in building a successful business is recruiting talent. A strong team can propel your business forward, whilst a weak one can hold you back. Identifying the right individuals to join your mission can be a game changer, and doing this right from the start sets the tone for your business culture and productivity. So where do you begin?

First, start by clearly defining the roles you need to fill. Each business is unique, and the positions you need will depend on your specific goals and operational needs. Break down the skill sets and qualifications necessary for each role. For a tech startup, for example, you might require software

CHAPTER 20: BUILDING A STRONG TEAM

developers, graphic designers, and digital marketers. For a retail business, sales personnel, inventory managers, and customer service representatives will be key. Being specific about these roles will save you time and help attract the right candidates.

Next, consider your company culture. This isn't just about choosing people who can do the job; it's about finding individuals who align with your company's values and vision. Hiring for cultural fit is essential because it fosters a more cohesive and productive working environment. Reflect on what defines your business culture: Is it innovation? Customer-centricity? Fast-paced decision-making? Once you have this framework, you can tailor your interview questions to ensure your candidates align with these values.

Now let's talk about the recruitment strategy. There are several methods you can use to find potential candidates. Start with your immediate network. Referrals from trusted sources can often yield high-quality candidates. Utilize social media platforms like LinkedIn to broadcast job openings and attract professionals who are actively looking for opportunities. Job boards and recruitment websites can also be effective, especially those that cater to your industry. Remember to craft compelling job postings that not only describe the role but also highlight the unique opportunities and benefits your company offers.

When it comes to the interview process, tailor your questions to evaluate both technical skills and cultural fit. Behavioral interview questions can help you understand how a candidate has handled past situations, giving you insight into their problem-solving abilities and teamwork skills. Ask about their experiences working on similar projects, how they managed tight deadlines, or how they navigated challenges and conflicts. A mix of situational and technical questions will help you get a well-rounded view of each candidate.

It's worth considering diverse hiring practices. Building a diverse team brings in multiple perspectives, fosters creativity, and equips your business to connect with a broader customer base. Actively seek out candidates from various backgrounds and experiences. This inclusivity can only strengthen your team and enrich the decision-making process within your business.

Compensation and benefits are another vital aspect of recruiting talent. While startups might not always offer the highest salaries, there are other ways to attract top talent. Consider offering equity, which can be a significant motivator for candidates who believe in your vision and want a stake in the company's success. Flexible working conditions, opportunities for growth, and a positive work environment are other factors that can make your offer more attractive.

Don't overlook the onboarding process. Once you've recruited your talent, it's essential to integrate them smoothly into your team. Provide comprehensive orientation sessions where new hires can learn about the company's mission, values, and goals. Assign mentors or buddies who can help them navigate their first few weeks. The quicker new employees understand their roles and the team dynamics, the quicker they can start contributing effectively.

As your business grows, you may find the need to recruit at different levels, from entry-level positions to executive roles. Developing a scalable recruitment process is crucial. Use applicant tracking systems (ATS) to manage your hiring pipeline efficiently. Automated systems can streamline the process, filtering candidates based on specific criteria and ensuring you never miss out on promising talent due to administrative overload.

Communication is key during the recruitment process. Keep candidates informed at each stage, whether they're moving forward or not. A positive recruitment experience can create goodwill for your business, even among those who don't join your team. They might still speak positively about your business and refer other talented individuals your way.

Hiring is as much about selling your company to the candidates as it is about evaluating them. Showcase the exciting projects they will work on, the impact they will make, and the team they will collaborate with. Express your passion and vision for the company. When candidates feel your enthusiasm and understand the mission they will be part of, they are more likely to invest emotionally in the role.

Lastly, always be looking for talent. The best candidates might not always come through a formal job advertisement. Keep your eyes open at industry events, networking opportunities, and even social gatherings. You never know when you might meet someone perfect for your team. Promote your company as an excellent place to work at every opportunity.

In summary, recruiting talent is an ongoing, dynamic process that requires a strategic approach. By clearly defining roles, prioritizing cultural fit, leveraging diverse recruitment strategies, and continually refining your processes, you'll build a robust team that can drive your business towards its million-dollar goal. Remember, your team is one of your most significant assets, and investing time and resources into finding the right people will pay off manifold as your business scales.

Team Dynamics and Leadership

Building a strong team isn't just about hiring the right people; it's about creating an environment where individuals can thrive and work toward a common goal. When you think about starting a million-dollar business over a weekend, the team dynamics you establish early on can make or break your success. Leadership in this context isn't about fancy titles or corner offices; it's about inspiring, guiding, and enabling your team to achieve collective greatness.

To start, let's talk about the importance of a shared vision. You can't expect people to rally behind you if they don't know where you're headed. Clearly articulate your business goals and how each team member's role fits into the bigger picture. Sharing this vision fosters a sense of purpose, turning a group of individuals into a cohesive unit. A unified vision also helps in making quicker decisions, essential when you're moving at the pace of a weekend startup.

While vision is critical, communication is the glue that holds your team together. Effective communication should be transparent, frequent, and multi-directional. It's not just about top-down directives but also about encouraging feedback and fostering an open dialogue. Create channels where everyone feels comfortable sharing their thoughts, be it through regular team meetings, chat platforms, or even an anonymous suggestion box. Clear communication eliminates ambiguity, ensuring everyone is on the same page and can act swiftly.

Leadership in a high-speed startup environment also demands adaptability. As a leader, you need to be fluid in your approach, willing to pivot strategies based on feedback and evolving conditions. This may mean quickly reassessing roles, shifting responsibilities, or even reevaluating the business model itself. By showing flexibility and a willingness to adapt, you inspire your team to remain agile and responsive, vital attributes for a fledgling business.

Now comes the tricky part: conflict resolution. Any group effort will inevitably encounter disagreements. How you handle these conflicts will set the tone for the team's morale and future interactions. Address issues head-on but with empathy. Understand the perspectives of those involved and work collaboratively to find solutions. Emphasizing a problem-solving mindset over blame or frustration can turn conflicts into opportunities for growth and learning.

Another key aspect of team dynamics is recognizing and nurturing individual strengths. Every team member brings a unique set of skills and experiences to the table. Leveraging these diversities rather than homogenizing efforts can lead to innovative solutions and a more robust team performance. It's essential to provide opportunities for professional growth, whether through mentorship, training, or challenges that push their boundaries. When people feel their strengths are acknowledged and nurtured, their engagement and productivity soar.

Leadership in this setting is also about leading by example. If you're asking your team to put in extra hours, show that you're willing to do the same. Demonstrating commitment, resilience, and a positive attitude can significantly influence your team's culture. People tend to emulate the behaviors they see from their leaders, so your actions can inspire a wave of collective effort and motivation.

Trust is another cornerstone of effective team dynamics. Building trust takes time, but it can be accelerated through consistent, reliable behavior. Trust your team to make decisions within their purview and avoid micromanaging. When people feel trusted, they are more likely to take ownership

CHAPTER 20: BUILDING A STRONG TEAM

of their roles and contribute more meaningfully to the team's objectives. Conversely, a lack of trust can stifle creativity and lead to a disengaged, disheartened team.

Encouraging a culture of accountability is equally important. In a fast-paced environment, there's little room for error, and accountability ensures everyone understands their responsibilities and the impact of their actions. Set clear expectations from the outset and use performance metrics to track progress. However, accountability should not be about blame but about learning and continuous improvement. Mistakes should be viewed as learning opportunities, fostering a culture where people feel safe to take risks and innovate.

Lastly, don't underestimate the power of appreciation and recognition. Highlighting small wins along the way can keep the team motivated and energized. Recognize individual and collective achievements publicly and promptly. A simple thank you can go a long way in maintaining high morale and a positive team spirit. After all, people are more likely to go the extra mile if they feel their efforts are valued and appreciated.

In summary, building a strong team in the context of a weekend startup involves more than just assembling a group of skilled individuals. It requires a shared vision, effective communication, adaptability, conflict resolution skills, recognition of individual strengths, leading by example, fostering trust, encouraging accountability, and appreciating contributions. Mastering these dynamics sets the stage for turning your entrepreneurial vision into reality. With the right team and leadership, the ambitious goal of starting a million-dollar business in 48 hours becomes not just feasible but inspiringly possible.

Chapter 21: Continuous Improvement

In any pursuit of building a million-dollar business, the concept of continuous improvement is paramount. This isn't just about making incremental changes; it's about fostering a mindset that's always looking for ways to enhance every aspect of your venture. Analyzing performance metrics critically will reveal where efficiencies can be gained and where strategies need tweaking. As market conditions fluctuate, adaptability becomes your strongest asset. Businesses that continually reassess and refine their approaches outpace the competition and sustain growth. Whether you're analyzing customer feedback or studying market trends, the goal is to create a flexible, responsive business model that can thrive in any environment. Remember, every small adjustment can compound into significant outcomes, positioning your business for long-term success and innovation.

Analyzing Performance

When it comes to launching and growing a million-dollar business in just 48 hours, the pace is unquestionably rapid. It's almost like a high-stakes game where every decision counts. But to keep the momentum going, analyzing performance becomes absolutely crucial. You might think of it as your business's regular health check-up. Without periodically checking how it's doing, you run the risk of drifting off course, making inefficient decisions, and potentially even failing. This section will delve deep into why analyzing performance is so vital and how you can do it effectively, ensuring your entrepreneurial journey continues on the right track.

CHAPTER 21: CONTINUOUS IMPROVEMENT

First and foremost, performance analysis helps you identify what's working and what's not. Imagine you're setting out on a cross-country road trip. Along the way, you'd frequently check your map or GPS to ensure you're on the right path. Similarly, in business, the metrics and performance indicators are your guideposts. By regularly reviewing these, you can quickly spot trends, good or bad, and adjust your strategy accordingly. This proactive approach ensures you're not just reacting to problems but anticipating them.

One of the simplest yet most effective methods of performance analysis is through Key Performance Indicators (KPIs). KPIs are quantifiable measures that gauge your business's performance against its objectives. For example, if your goal is to drive sales, relevant KPIs might include monthly sales revenue, conversion rates, and average transaction value. Tracking these KPIs on a regular basis will help you pinpoint exactly where you need to focus your efforts to boost performance.

While KPIs are critical, they aren't the end-all and be-all of performance analysis. Qualitative feedback is just as important. Customer reviews and employee feedback can provide invaluable insights that numbers alone can't offer. For instance, repeated customer comments about long delivery times could indicate a supply chain issue that needs addressing. Similarly, employee feedback about feeling overwhelmed might signal the need for additional resources or better processes.

Data analytics tools can further elevate your performance analysis. Tools like Google Analytics, customer relationship management (CRM) systems, and various financial software can automate the data collection process and provide you with real-time insights. With these tools, you can quickly generate reports, identify patterns, and make data-driven decisions. The power of these tools lies in their ability to organize vast amounts of data into actionable insights, making your job considerably easier and more effective.

Setting up regular performance review sessions is another vital part of the puzzle. Create a schedule for reviewing your KPIs, be it weekly, bi-weekly, or monthly. These sessions should be comprehensive, covering all aspects of your operation—from sales and marketing to supply chain logistics and customer service. During these reviews, encourage an open dialogue among your team members. They're often the closest to the action and can provide invaluable insights that might get lost in the data.

Moreover, it's essential not to get bogged down by vanity metrics. While it's tempting to focus on numbers that look good on paper, such as social media likes or website traffic, these metrics don't always correlate with your bottom line. Focus on metrics that directly impact your business goals. For instance, instead of focusing solely on website traffic, look at conversion rates and average order values—these figures have a direct impact on your revenue.

The importance of a feedback loop cannot be overstated. This is a system where the outputs of a process are used as inputs for future actions. In simpler terms, it's about learning from your performance metrics to make better decisions moving forward. Once you identify areas that need improvement, take immediate action to address these issues. Then, reassess your performance to see if those changes had the desired effect. This loop should be continuous, as ongoing refinement is crucial for long-term success.

Benchmarking is another valuable exercise. It involves comparing your business performance against industry standards or competitors. This can provide a context for your performance metrics and help you understand where you stand in the bigger picture. For example, if your customer acquisition cost is higher than the industry average, it might indicate inefficiencies in your marketing strategies. Keep an eye on your competitors, observe their strategies, and understand what makes them successful. You can then integrate these insights into your own business model.

Keeping documentation of your performance reviews and the decisions made can be immensely beneficial. This creates a historical record that you can reference to see how decisions impacted your business over time. It's like a journal for your business, capturing both successes and lessons learned. Over time, this documentation can help you identify long-term trends and make more informed strategic decisions.

Additionally, be prepared to pivot based on your performance analysis. Flexibility is one of the hallmarks of a successful entrepreneur. If the data clearly indicates that your current strategy isn't working, don't be afraid to

CHAPTER 21: CONTINUOUS IMPROVEMENT

make significant changes. This might involve shifting your target market, reevaluating your business model, or even completely overhauling your product offerings. The quicker you can adapt, the better your chances of achieving sustained success.

Lastly, share your performance results with your stakeholders, whether they are employees, investors, or partners. Transparency builds trust and fosters a culture of accountability. When everyone is aware of how the business is performing and what challenges lie ahead, they're more likely to be invested in the success of the business. This collective effort can drive your business forward more effectively than any solo effort.

In conclusion, analyzing performance is not just a task to check off your to-do list; it's an ongoing process that can make or break your business. By paying attention to both quantitative KPIs and qualitative feedback, leveraging the power of data analytics tools, and maintaining a constant feedback loop, you can ensure your business stays on course. Moreover, benchmarking, documenting, and remaining flexible in your strategies further position you for long-term success. Remember, the road to a million-dollar business isn't a straight line; it's filled with twists and turns. But with robust performance analysis, you'll navigate it successfully, making smart, informed decisions at every step.

Adapting to Market Changes

In the dynamic world of entrepreneurship, the only constant is change. Having a great idea and a solid plan is fundamental, but when market landscapes shift, your ability to adapt is what distinguishes an enduring success from a fleeting trend. Market conditions fluctuate due to a myriad of factors— economic cycles, consumer preferences, technological advancements, and even unexpected events like pandemics. Your agility in responding to these changes can spell the difference between thriving and merely surviving.

Understanding customer behavior is crucial. Consumer preferences evolve, and so should your offerings. Today's hot product might be tomorrow's forgotten fad. To stay ahead, immerse yourself in continuous market research.

This doesn't mean allocating enormous resources but rather instilling a habit of constant learning and observing. Use social media, surveys, and customer feedback to keep a pulse on what your audience desires. Be receptive to feedback and ready to pivot your strategies when necessary.

Technological advancements also play a significant role in market changes. New tools and platforms can shift the competitive landscape overnight. Staying attuned to technological innovations will enable you to harness their potential before your competitors do. This might involve adopting new software, integrating innovative marketing techniques, or simply using technology to streamline operations.

Economic conditions are another variable to consider. A booming economy creates opportunities for expansion, while a downturn may necessitate cost-cutting measures or shifts in revenue models. Diversifying your products or services can mitigate risks associated with economic fluctuations. Don't place all your bets on a single offering; instead, think about how you can leverage your core competencies to explore new avenues.

Competitor analysis, though often overlooked, is invaluable. Keep an eye on your competitors—not just to replicate their successes but to learn from their failures. Competitor moves can provide insights into emerging trends and market demands. This, in turn, helps in positioning your business more favorably within the market. Remember, acquiring knowledge from others' experiences accelerates your learning curve without paying the price of experimenting from scratch.

Flexibility in your business model is essential. Certain strategies that work perfectly under one set of market conditions may become obsolete when the landscape shifts. For instance, during economic downturns, subscription-based models might be more sustainable than one-time purchases. On the flip side, during a booming economy, premium pricing on exclusive offerings can maximize profits. Explore various revenue models and understand how each one performs under different market conditions.

Building a strong network can also be beneficial in adapting to market changes. Connecting with other entrepreneurs, mentors, and industry experts provides a platform for sharing insights and strategies. Your network can offer support, guidance, and opportunities during uncertain times. This collective wisdom enriches your perspective and helps you anticipate and respond to changes more effectively.

Forecasting and anticipating change is another crucial practice. While you can't predict the future with certainty, you can prepare for different scenarios. Implementing processes for regular review and adjustment of your business plans ensures that you remain nimble. This could involve setting quarterly goals and assessing your performance against them, as well as tweaking your strategies to align with the latest market trends.

Marketing strategies must evolve as well. The channels and methods you use to reach your audience might not always yield the same results. Continually experiment with new marketing tactics, whether it's leveraging new social media platforms, adopting innovative content strategies, or refining your advertising campaigns. Adaptation in marketing not only keeps your brand relevant but also uncovers new avenues for growth.

Adaptability in customer service can't be overlooked. Ensuring that your customer support evolves in response to market changes can provide a significant competitive advantage. This could mean adopting new communication channels, personalizing interactions, or simply improving response times. In ever-changing markets, exceptional customer service can become a differentiator that keeps your business afloat and thriving.

Financial flexibility is equally important. Keep an eye on your cash flow and maintain a reserve that allows you to pivot when necessary. This safety net can prove invaluable during periods of market volatility. It's also wise to explore diverse revenue streams that can buffer against downturns in any single area of your business.

Market changes can sometimes call for innovation in your products or services. This could be as simple as adding new features based on customer feedback or as complex as pivoting your core offering to meet a new demand. Encourage a culture of innovation within your team. Allow room for creative thinking and experimentation, and don't be afraid to take calculated risks.

Finally, mindset matters. Adapting to market changes requires resilience and a positive outlook. Embrace challenges as opportunities for growth rather than obstacles. By maintaining a flexible mindset, you can navigate uncertain waters with confidence and emerge stronger. Remember, every successful entrepreneur has faced the challenge of adaptation; it's a critical part of the journey.

To conclude, the ability to adapt to market changes is not merely an asset but a necessity for sustained success. By staying informed, flexible, and proactive, you can navigate the ebbs and flows of the market landscape. Embrace change as an inevitable and exciting aspect of your entrepreneurial journey. Your resilience and adaptability will not only help you survive but thrive in the ever-evolving business world.

Chapter 22: Managing Stress and Burnout

Entrepreneurship, while exhilarating, often brings an intense level of stress that can lead to burnout if not managed properly. As you dive into launching and scaling your million-dollar business within 48 hours, it's crucial to prioritize your mental health and maintain a harmonious work-life balance. Incorporate regular breaks, set realistic goals, and don't hesitate to seek support from mental health resources when needed. Remember, the key to sustained success isn't just about pushing through but also about pacing yourself and recharging. Effective stress management can keep your passion alive and prevent burnout, enabling you to continue innovating and driving your business forward with clarity and vigor.

Work-Life Balance Tips

Achieving a harmonious work-life balance is critical, especially for those who are diving headfirst into entrepreneurial ventures while managing other life responsibilities. The hustle and grind can feel endless, but taking mindful steps can ensure you thrive without succumbing to burnout.

First and foremost, setting boundaries is crucial. Establishing clear work hours can help delineate between business time and personal time. If you're working from home, create a dedicated workspace. A clear physical separation can help mentally switch between work and relaxation modes.

Moreover, don't underestimate the power of saying "no." As exciting as new opportunities can be, overcommitment is a fast track to burnout. Prioritize tasks and opportunities that genuinely align with your business goals and personal well-being. Remember, quality over quantity is a mantra that pays off in the long run.

Taking regular breaks is essential. Short, frequent breaks throughout your workday can refresh your mind, reduce stress, and increase productivity. Additionally, practice the Pomodoro Technique—working in focused intervals of 25 minutes followed by a 5-minute break—to maintain high efficiency without overwhelming yourself.

Physical activity also plays an indispensable role in maintaining a balanced life. Incorporating even a short 20-minute workout into your daily routine can help reduce stress, boost mood, and improve cognitive function. Whether it's a morning yoga session, a brisk walk during lunch, or a workout at the gym, find a form of exercise that you enjoy and can consistently maintain.

Don't forget the importance of nutrition. Consuming balanced meals with plenty of fruits, vegetables, whole grains, and lean proteins can keep your energy levels steady and your mind sharp. Avoid excessive caffeine and sugar, which can lead to crashes and mood swings. Always keep a water bottle at your desk to stay hydrated throughout the day.

Sleep is another cornerstone of effective work-life balance. A well-rested entrepreneur is far more capable and creative. Aim for 7-9 hours of quality sleep each night, and try to maintain a consistent sleep schedule, even on weekends. Create a pre-sleep routine that signals your body it's time to wind down, such as reading a book or practicing relaxation exercises.

Time management tools can be lifesavers. Utilize apps and planners to keep track of tasks and deadlines. Tools like Trello, Asana, or even a simple Google Calendar can help you organize your days and prevent last-minute chaos. Having a clear plan can reduce anxiety about what needs to be done and when.

Mindfulness and meditation can also be powerful allies. Spending just a few minutes each day in meditation can lower stress levels and increase your ability to focus. There are numerous apps like Headspace or Calm that offer guided sessions ranging from 3 to 30 minutes. Integrating mindfulness into your routine can aid in making thoughtful, balanced decisions in both work and personal spheres.

Don't forget to seek support when you need it. Surround yourself with a

CHAPTER 22: MANAGING STRESS AND BURNOUT

strong network of family, friends, or fellow entrepreneurs who can provide both emotional support and practical advice. Sometimes, just having someone to talk to can alleviate the mental load and offer new perspectives.

It's equally important to allocate time for activities that replenish you. Hobbies, leisure activities, and spending quality time with loved ones nourish your soul and provide a much-needed break from business pressures. Whether it's reading a novel, playing a musical instrument, or simply watching a movie with family, ensure you're dedicating time to these pursuits.

Another fundamental aspect is setting realistic goals. While it's essential to dream big, breaking your massive goals into smaller, achievable tasks can help you maintain momentum without overwhelming yourself. Celebrate these small wins to keep your motivation high.

Keep in mind, flexibility is key. Life is unpredictable, and sometimes your best-laid plans will need adjustments. Adaptability prevents the stress of rigidly sticking to plans that no longer serve your current situation. Embrace the flow and make adjustments as necessary.

Regularly reviewing and reassessing your workload and priorities can also be beneficial. Take the time weekly or bi-weekly to evaluate what's working and what isn't. This habit can help you stay aligned with both your long-term goals and immediate needs, allowing you to make informed adjustments.

Communication with your team or business partners is indispensable too. Keeping everyone on the same page regarding workloads, deadlines, and expectations can mitigate misunderstandings and prevent unnecessary stress. Whether through regular meetings or collaborative tools, maintain open lines of communication.

Lastly, don't shy away from professional help if needed. Therapists, coaches, or business consultants can offer strategies and perspectives that you might not have considered. Sometimes, an outside view can bring clarity and direction that's hard to achieve on your own.

Incorporating these tips into your daily routine can transform your entrepreneurial journey from a stressful endeavor into a fulfilling, balanced lifestyle. Remember, achieving work-life balance isn't about perfection but about making continuous, mindful adjustments to foster well-being and success.

Mental Health Resources

It's evident that entrepreneurship comes with its share of challenges, often leading to stress and burnout. The mental toll can be hefty, especially when you're juggling multiple responsibilities. Here, we delve into essential mental health resources that every entrepreneur, side hustler, or business owner should be aware of. Remember, mental resilience is as crucial as any business strategy you adopt.

Sometimes, the best way to manage your mental health is by proactively engaging with it. Apps like Headspace and Calm offer guided meditation and mindfulness exercises that can help you stay grounded. Such tools are convenient and can be accessed anytime, making them ideal for busy entrepreneurs. Just 10 minutes a day can significantly improve your mental clarity and emotional well-being.

Consider joining a support group. Whether it's an online forum or a local meet-up, connecting with others in similar situations can be immensely helpful. Platforms like Meetup or Facebook Groups host communities where entrepreneurs share their struggles and solutions. Engaging with a support network combats the isolation that often accompanies entrepreneurship, providing you with a sense of camaraderie and encouragement.

You might also want to explore therapy or counseling. Services like BetterHelp and Talkspace offer online counseling that fits into your schedule. Professional mental health support can offer personalized strategies to manage stress and prevent burnout. It's essential to debunk the stigma around therapy—acknowledging you need help is a sign of strength, not weakness.

Physical exercise is another cornerstone of mental health. Regular physical activity releases endorphins, improving your mood and energy levels. You don't need a fancy gym membership to stay active; even a brisk walk or a quick home workout session can do wonders. Activities like yoga and Pilates, accessible via platforms like YouTube or specialized apps, combine physical movement with mindfulness, further enhancing your mental equilibrium.

Don't underestimate the value of proper nutrition. A balanced diet can significantly affect how you feel and perform. Foods rich in Omega-3 fatty acids, whole grains, and leafy greens are particularly effective at boosting brain health. Stay hydrated and consider reducing caffeine and alcohol, which can exacerbate anxiety and stress.

Time management tools can also help reduce stress. Apps like Trello and Asana assist in organizing your tasks, ensuring you prioritize effectively. When you allocate specific times for work, breaks, and personal activities, you create a structure that reduces overwhelm. The Pomodoro Technique, which involves working in focused intervals followed by short breaks, can enhance productivity while giving your brain the necessary downtime.

Maintaining a strong work-life balance is another vital aspect of mental health. Make sure to set boundaries between your work and personal life. Designate a specific workspace and limit your working hours to prevent your job from spilling into your personal time. Engage in hobbies and activities that you enjoy outside of work, whether that's reading, cooking, or spending time with loved ones. Moments of joy and relaxation are essential for recharging your mental batteries.

Sleep hygiene should not be overlooked. Quality sleep is crucial for cognitive function, emotional stability, and overall health. Aim for at least 7-8 hours of sleep per night. Establish a bedtime routine that helps signal to your body that it's time to wind down. This could include activities like reading a book, listening to calming music, or practicing deep-breathing exercises.

Another resource at your disposal is literature. There are numerous books on mental health and resilience that can provide insight and strategies. Titles like "The Upside of Stress" by Kelly McGonigal or "Atomic Habits" by James Clear offer valuable perspectives on managing stress and building productive habits. Make reading a part of your daily routine, even if it's just a chapter a day. Knowledge can be empowering and offer new ways to approach your challenges.

Podcasts are another fantastic resource. There are several series dedicated to mental health, mindfulness, and entrepreneurship. Listening to experts discuss these topics can offer new strategies and give you a sense of community. Podcasts like "The Tim Ferriss Show" or "How I Built This" often delve into the mental hurdles faced by successful entrepreneurs and provide actionable advice.

Community engagement is also critical. Volunteering or engaging in community services can offer a sense of fulfillment and perspective. When you contribute to something bigger than yourself, it often mitigates stress by shifting your focus outward. Find causes or organizations that resonate with you and contribute your time or skills. This act of giving can provide emotional rewards that far outweigh the time invested.

Lastly, don't overlook the power of laughter and leisure. Humor and light-hearted activities are excellent for alleviating stress. Watch a comedy show, hang out with friends who make you laugh, or engage in activities that bring you joy. Laughter is a proven stress reliever, and integrating fun into your life will make your entrepreneurial journey more enjoyable and sustainable.

In summary, managing stress and burnout requires a multifaceted approach. Utilize tools like meditation apps, time management software, and online counseling services. Engage in physical activities, eat a balanced diet, and maintain a healthy sleep routine. Read, listen to podcasts, and involve yourself in community activities to gain new perspectives and build resilience. And most importantly, find joy in the journey by integrating humor and leisure into your life. Your mental health is your most valuable asset—nurture it, and it will serve you well on your path to entrepreneurial success.

Chapter 23: Networking and Partnerships

Networking and partnerships aren't just buzzwords—they're the keystone of any thriving business, especially when you're racing against the clock to build your million-dollar venture. Start by identifying key players in your industry and reaching out for mutually beneficial relationships. Strategic connections can open doors you didn't even know existed, offering insights, resources, and opportunities that can propel you past stumbling blocks. Don't shy away from collaboration; leverage it. Shared expertise and pooled resources can double your strength, allowing you to focus on scaling quicker and more efficiently. Ultimately, the partnerships you form can be the catalysts that elevate your side hustle from a fledgling idea to a significant market contender.

Building Strategic Relationships

When it comes to building a million-dollar business in such a short span, like over a weekend, your network can be just as valuable as your skills or the product itself. Strategic relationships are not just about knowing a lot of people; they're about knowing the right people and, more importantly, nurturing these connections meaningfully. Think of it as planting a garden. You don't just scatter seeds; you care for each plant so it grows and flourishes.

First and foremost, quality trumps quantity. You could attend countless networking events or join numerous social media groups, but if you're not making quality connections, you're wasting your time. Aim to build relationships with individuals who share your values, understand your vision, and can offer resources, advice, or connections that are mutually beneficial. Finding these individuals might require research, targeted networking, and a bit of patience.

One powerful method is to start within your own existing network. No matter who you are, you likely have access to people who can introduce you to others. Friends, family, colleagues, and even acquaintances may already have valuable connections that just need a little nurturing. Don't underestimate the power of a warm introduction. A referral from someone within your inner circle can carry significant weight and open doors that might otherwise remain closed.

You'll also want to leverage the power of social media strategically. Platforms like LinkedIn, Twitter, and even Instagram can be gold mines for finding and connecting with thought leaders in your industry. However, don't just send random connection requests. Personalize your messages and explain why you're interested in connecting. Mention common interests, mutual connections, or shared goals to make your outreach more meaningful. The goal is to establish a rapport and not simply collect contacts.

Another key aspect is to engage in professional groups relevant to your industry. Look for forums, online communities, and local meetups where you can meet like-minded individuals. Sharing your knowledge and providing value within these spaces can help you gain credibility and trust. Be active, ask questions, provide answers, and contribute to discussions. Over time, people will recognize your expertise and be more willing to collaborate with you.

Networking events, both virtual and in-person, remain invaluable for building strategic relationships. Whether it's a conference, a workshop, or a business mixer, attend with a clear objective. Know what you want to achieve, whether it's meeting potential clients, partners, or mentors. Don't aim to talk to everyone; instead, focus on forging a few deeper connections. Prepare a concise personal pitch, but also be an excellent listener. People remember how you make them feel, so focus on creating genuine, sincere interactions rather than pitching incessantly.

Mentorship can play a significant role in your networking strategy. Identifying and connecting with a mentor who has been through the entrepreneurial journey you're embarking on can provide invaluable insights and shortcuts through common pitfalls. Be respectful of their time and start by seeking small bits of advice or guidance. Show appreciation and also be willing to provide value in return, no matter how small it might seem. The mentor-mentee relationship should be a two-way street.

Furthermore, consider the importance of strategic partnerships. These are often business relationships where both parties agree to cooperate for mutual benefit. If you're starting a new business, finding partners who can help you scale quickly is crucial. Look for complementary businesses where you each can offer something the other needs, creating a win-win situation. For example, a local bakery could partner with a coffee shop to offer exclusive deals, sharing customer bases and increasing exposure for both. Such partnerships can include co-branding, joint marketing efforts, or even shared physical spaces.

Collaborations are a subset of strategic partnerships but can be more project-based or temporary. Think of co-hosting an event, co-authoring a blog post, or launching a combined product. Collaboration opens you to new audiences and allows you to share resources. Both parties can harness the power of these collective efforts to maximize reach and impact. Plus, working with others brings in fresh perspectives and ideas, often pushing you to perform better and think more creatively.

To maintain and grow these strategic relationships, consistent follow-up is vital. After meeting someone new, send a follow-up message within a few days to recap your conversation and express your interest in staying in touch. Make it a habit to check in periodically, even if it's just a friendly email or a social media comment. Share useful articles, congratulate them on their milestones, and find ways to keep the relationship alive without it becoming transactional.

Lastly, always approach these relationships with a mindset of giving rather than taking. The most influential networkers are those who give value first, whether through sharing knowledge, making introductions, or offering help. When you provide value without immediately expecting something in return, you build a solid foundation of trust and goodwill. This mindset can transform simple connections into long-lasting, mutually beneficial relationships.

In conclusion, building strategic relationships is an art that requires intention, effort, and authenticity. It is not about collecting as many business cards as possible but about forging partnerships that can help your venture thrive. By focusing on the quality of your interactions, leveraging social media smartly, and consistently providing value, you'll create a robust network that supports your business growth. Remember, the relationships you cultivate now can pay massive dividends in the future.

Collaborating for Success

In the dynamic world of business, no one truly achieves monumental success alone. Collaboration isn't just a buzzword; it's an essential ingredient in the recipe for your million-dollar business. Whether you're a fresh-faced student or a seasoned entrepreneur, harnessing the power of partnerships can propel your venture forward far quicker than going it alone.

Begin by identifying key individuals and organizations that align with your business goals. Think about who can complement your strengths and shore up your weaknesses. For instance, if you're great at product development but lack marketing expertise, seek out someone who excels in that realm. This isn't just about finding someone to do the work you can't; it's about creating a synergy that multiplies your capabilities.

Networking events, both online and offline, are fertile grounds for finding such collaborators. Attend industry conferences, join relevant social media groups, or participate in webinars. Regardless of where you encounter potential partners, make sure to communicate your vision clearly. People are more inclined to collaborate when they understand and believe in your mission.

The first step to successful collaboration is building trust. Open communication is crucial. Be transparent about your expectations, timelines, and goals from the outset. A clear, mutually beneficial arrangement paves the way for a smoother partnership. Leveraging tools like shared digital workspaces can

CHAPTER 23: NETWORKING AND PARTNERSHIPS

keep everyone on the same page, fostering a sense of unity and purpose.

Don't shy away from thinking outside the box when it comes to potential collaborators. Strategic partnerships can include influencers who can promote your product, suppliers who can offer better rates for raw materials, or even fellow entrepreneurs who might want to cross-promote products or services. Each partnership should be analyzed for its contribution to your business's ultimate goals. Remember, the aim is to create win-win scenarios.

Another avenue for collaboration is within local business communities and support networks. Many cities have business incubators or networking clubs that provide resources, mentorship, and connections. These platforms can offer invaluable guidance and might even help you find your next big collaborator. Take advantage of every opportunity to build relationships within these circles.

If you're coming from a non-business background, leveraging these relationships becomes even more critical. Business acumen can often be borrowed, so don't hesitate to partner with someone who has industry knowledge you lack. This can accelerate your learning curve and make it easier to navigate challenges that crop up early in your business journey.

Financial collaborations are also worth exploring. Pooling resources with one or more partners can unlock capital investment, making it easier to hit those ambitious targets. Look into joint ventures or collaborative crowdfunding campaigns. These approaches distribute risk and can provide the financial backing needed to scale operations quickly.

Collaborating for success also involves embracing modern technological tools that facilitate teamwork. Project management platforms, video conferencing software, and collaborative cloud services streamline communication and operational efficiency. Utilize these tools to break down geographical barriers, opening up a global pool of potential collaborators. Always stay open to partnerships that might not look conventional but offer significant strategic advantage.

As your business grows, continuously reassess your collaborative agreements. Not every partnership will stand the test of time, and that's okay. Ending a collaboration on good terms is just as important as starting one.

Evaluate the contributions and outcomes regularly, adjusting the terms as necessary or, if beneficial, parting ways amicably.

Furthermore, fostering a culture of collaboration within your own team can dramatically amplify results. Encourage cross-functional teams where marketing, development, and customer service experts work hand-in-hand. When employees feel they are part of a collaborative and cohesive unit, morale and productivity soar. Regular team-building activities and open-door policies for feedback can nurture this culture effectively.

Be mindful that collaboration is a two-way street. Just as you seek help, be prepared to offer assistance to others. Whether it's through mentorship, sharing expertise, or providing resources, supporting fellow entrepreneurs can build a network that returns the favor. These acts of generosity often lead to lasting relationships and reciprocal business opportunities.

One aspect to keep in mind is the legal framework surrounding collaborations. Establishing clear contracts and understanding the legal implications is mandatory. Whether formalizing a partnership, joint venture, or even simple service agreements, always seek legal advice to avoid complications down the line.

In essence, collaborating for success means weaving a web of supportive, strategic alliances that help propel your business to new heights. It's about finding the right people, fostering a culture of trust and mutual benefit, and leveraging each other's strengths to achieve goals that would be impossible to reach alone. Remember, every successful entrepreneur stands not just on their own strengths, but on the shoulders of those they collaborate with.

Keep an open mind, always be on the lookout for potential partners, and don't hesitate to take the first step in reaching out. By embracing collaboration, you not only expand your capabilities but also create a network of allies who are as invested in your success as you are.

Harness the collective power of collaborative efforts and watch your million-dollar business idea take flight. With the right people by your side, there's no limit to what you can achieve, even within the short span of a weekend.

Chapter 24: Case Studies of Weekend Success

In just 48 hours, countless entrepreneurs have transformed weekend projects into thriving businesses. Consider the story of Emily, a stay-at-home mom who launched an artisanal soap company from her kitchen. Within two days, she leveraged social media to secure her first 100 customers. Or take Mark, a college student who developed an app to enhance study habits. Through targeted marketing, he gained 1,000 users before Monday classes resumed. These stories are not anomalies; they are blueprints showcasing the power of focused effort, rapid validation, and strategic execution. Learning from these cases provides invaluable lessons and underscores the principle that with the right approach, you can indeed start a million-dollar business over a weekend.

Real Stories and Lessons Learned

Diving into the realm of weekend success stories offers valuable insights into the dos and don'ts of launching a business within a tight timeframe. With these real-life experiences, we can draw not only inspiration but also practical lessons that translate into actionable advice for aspiring entrepreneurs.

Take the story of Jane, a stay-at-home mother who transformed her passion for baking into a profitable cupcake business. Jane's journey began on a Friday night when she decided to test her cupcake recipes at a local farmers' market over the weekend. Her cupcakes sold out within two hours, validating her idea. In those 48 hours, she not only made significant sales but also garnered a customer base that would follow her to her first brick-and-mortar store.

The key takeaway from Jane's story isn't just that she turned a hobby into a business. It's the way she leveraged community events, tested her products in a real market setting, and took quick action based on immediate feedback. Jane's story underscores the importance of being flexible and ready to pivot based on customer reactions.

Then there's Tom, a college student who utilized his coding skills to create a simple but effective budgeting app. By Saturday evening, Tom had a working prototype and decided to place an ad on a student bulletin board. The app's popularity spiked, and by Sunday, he had over 500 downloads. This instant validation pushed him to refine and eventually monetize the app.

Tom's experience demonstrates the importance of rapid prototyping and direct outreach. Instead of waiting for a perfect product, Tom's willingness to launch a basic version proved pivotal. Immediate market entry allowed him to gather user feedback and improve the app swiftly. Timing, as Tom's case shows, can be just as crucial as the product itself.

Consider the narrative of Raj, an IT professional who spotted a gap in his industry's training resources. Over one weekend, he created a series of online tutorials aimed at helping newcomers navigate complex software tools. By leveraging his professional network and social media, Raj promoted his tutorials, amassing a significant following. These tutorials eventually led to a full-fledged training business.

Raj's story highlights the incredible power of tapping into existing networks. His initial success was not just a result of his expertise but also his ability to engage and mobilize a community that trusted him. His journey teaches us that who you know can often be as essential as what you know.

Emily's leap into the pet accessories market offers another compelling case study. Working a corporate job during the week, Emily spent her weekends designing unique pet collars. She used social media platforms to share her creations and generate buzz. With the help of influencer partnerships, Emily's collars became a trending item. Her story is a testament to the vital role of modern marketing techniques and the influence of social media.

The moral here is clear: leveraging current digital tools can catapult your business from obscurity to trendiness in no time. Emily's use of social media influencers broadened her reach exponentially and built a loyal customer base that supported her growth into a full-time entrepreneur.

Not all weekend ventures meet with immediate success, and that's a critical lesson as well. Michael's attempt to start a food delivery service didn't gain traction initially. However, the feedback he received was invaluable. By paying attention to customer concerns—like delivery speed and food quality—he reworked his service and relaunched. The second time around, he found success.

Michael's journey underlines the importance of resilience and iteration. Initial failure provided him with essential data points to refine his business model. His eventual success was built on the lessons learned from those early setbacks.

Whether it's baking, coding, training, designing, or delivering—these stories share common threads of swift action, market validation, and the ability to adapt. Each narrative illustrates that success doesn't necessarily stem from following a single perfect strategy but rather from a series of well-informed, timely decisions.

Let's now focus on some tangible lessons surfaced by these stories:

- **Start Small, Dream Big:** Many weekend success stories began with a modest goal—to test a product or idea. Big dreams are fulfilled through manageable, small steps. Jane and her cupcakes didn't launch an empire overnight; they started with a local market.
- **Emphasize Speed:** Rapidly bringing an idea to market allows for quick validation, as seen in Tom's app launch. Procrastination can stymie progress. Acting quickly helps identify what works and what doesn't.
- **Leverage Your Network:** Raj's professional network was instrumental in his initial success. Building and utilizing networks can provide a wider audience, useful feedback, and essential support.
- **Embrace Social Media:** Emily's savvy use of social media created buzz around her pet collars. Leveraging digital platforms enables marketing

to a broad audience without the need for hefty budgets.
- **Iterate Based on Feedback:** Don't be discouraged by initial setbacks. Michael's resilience and willingness to iterate his food delivery service, based on customer feedback, ultimately led to success.

Each of these examples empowers us with both inspiration and actionable insights. They remind us that the crux of turning a weekend idea into a thriving business lies in swift execution, relentless feedback incorporation, and leveraging available resources, whether that's a community network, digital platform, or sheer grit and resilience.

As you prepare to embark on your weekend venture, keep these stories and lessons close. Consider that every entrepreneur started somewhere, often with a simple, executable idea and a relentless drive to see it succeed. The realm of possibilities is bound only by the limits of your imagination and willingness to act.

Remember, it's about taking that first action, learning fast, and pivoting when necessary. The journey you start over a weekend can evolve into a lifetime of entrepreneurial success, just as it did for Jane, Tom, Raj, Emily, and Michael.

Common Pitfalls and How to Avoid Them

While embarking on a weekend business venture sounds exhilarating, it's crucial to recognize that certain pitfalls can derail even the most passionate entrepreneurs. Understanding these common mistakes and how to avoid them is essential for anyone looking to achieve the same level of weekend success as those in the case studies.

One frequent pitfall is underestimating the importance of thorough research and preparation. Many aspiring entrepreneurs rush into their ventures without fully grasping their market, resulting in misguided efforts and eventual failure. To avoid this, spend ample time analyzing your target audience and competitors. Knowing your audience helps you tailor products or services that meet their needs, while a thorough competitor analysis reveals gaps you can exploit. It may seem time-consuming, but this initial groundwork is paramount.

Another common issue is an overambitious scope. Entrepreneurs, brimming with enthusiasm, often tackle too many ideas at once, leading to diluted efforts and subpar execution. To sidestep this, focus on a Minimum Viable Product (MVP) that allows you to test the waters without spreading your resources too thin. By concentrating on core functionalities first, you can iteratively improve based on real-world feedback.

Financial mismanagement is another pitfall that can cripple a budding business. Even with a fantastic idea, poor budgeting or overlooking hidden costs can quickly drain resources. Establishing a clear financial plan that includes all potential expenses, from marketing to logistics, is crucial. Tracking expenses closely and avoiding unnecessary spending will help you stay afloat until your business starts generating revenue.

Legal missteps also pose a significant risk. Ignoring the necessary legal and administrative steps can result in fines, lawsuits, or even the shutdown of your operation. Ensure you select the right business structure, register your enterprise, and familiarize yourself with pertinent regulations. Don't cut corners; investing time in legalities now prevents costly complications down the road.

Failing to adapt to feedback is a surprisingly common mistake among entrepreneurs. Many become attached to their initial ideas and resist changes suggested by early customers. To avoid this, develop a mindset of continuous improvement. View feedback as valuable insights rather than criticisms. By iterating your product or service based on user feedback, you enhance its appeal and functionality, driving greater customer satisfaction and loyalty.

Branding missteps are another area where new businesses often falter. A strong brand identity distinguishes you from competitors and communicates your business values effectively. Spending too little time on branding elements like your logo, tagline, and overall visual identity can result in a forgettable and unappealing presence. Invest in crafting a brand that resonates with your target audience and clearly reflects your mission and value proposition.

Underestimating the power of a robust online presence is another pitfall. In today's digital age, having a functional and attractive website is non-negotiable. Don't cut corners on your site's design or user experience. Additionally, leverage social media platforms to engage with your audience, announce updates, and create a sense of community around your brand. The more touchpoints you establish with potential customers, the easier it becomes to build a loyal customer base.

An often-ignored yet critical aspect is the launch strategy. Many entrepreneurs think launching a business is just about going live. In reality, having a carefully crafted launch plan can make all the difference. It includes pre-launch marketing, influencer partnerships, and strategic timing. A smooth and well-publicized launch sets the tone for sustained interest and sales momentum.

Another subtle but debilitating pitfall is poor time management. Balancing a full-time job or other commitments with a side hustle requires meticulous planning. Failing to allocate time properly can lead to burnout or substandard work. Use productivity tools and block out specific hours dedicated solely to your venture. Being organized not only keeps the business running smoothly but also helps in maintaining your personal well-being.

Customer acquisition is another area that can trip up new entrepreneurs. Many pour time and money into ineffective marketing channels without analyzing their ROI. Identify where your target customers spend their time and tailor your marketing strategies accordingly. Whether it's social media advertising, email marketing, or networking events, ensure every dollar spent is backed by measurable outcomes.

It's equally essential to prepare for scale. Early success can lead to complacency, and without scalable processes in place, rapid growth can cause operational chaos. Invest in systems and tools that streamline tasks like order processing, customer service, and inventory management. Automating repetitive tasks not only saves time but also ensures consistency and quality.

Finally, managing stress and avoiding burnout is vital. The excitement of launching a new business can lead to neglecting personal well-being. Make it a priority to take breaks, exercise, and maintain a social life outside of your entrepreneurial endeavors. Managing your mental health is not just about avoiding burnout; it hugely impacts your decision-making, creativity, and overall productivity.

In summary, while the journey to a million-dollar weekend success is thrilling, it requires a well-thought-out approach to navigate the common pitfalls. Through meticulous research, focused efforts, prudent financial management, legal diligence, adaptive feedback loops, strong branding, a strategic online presence, a detailed launch plan, efficient time management, targeted customer acquisition, scalable operations, and good mental health practices, you can steer clear of these pitfalls and set your business on a path to success. Stay focused, adaptable, and dedicated, and you'll find that the goal of creating a million-dollar business in 48 hours is not just a dream but an achievable reality.

Chapter 25: The Road Ahead

As you look forward to scaling the heights of entrepreneurial success, it's crucial to set long-term goals and plan for sustainable growth. Building a million-dollar business in 48 hours is just the beginning, but maintaining and expanding that success requires ongoing commitment and strategic planning. Think about where you want your business to be in one, five, and even ten years—what milestones will mark your journey? You'll need to continually adapt, innovate, and stay ahead of the market trends to ensure that your business doesn't just survive but thrives. Focus on establishing a solid foundation that can support future endeavors, and never stop seeking opportunities for improvement and expansion. By staying proactive and maintaining a clear vision, you're paving the road ahead for not just success, but lasting impact.

Setting Long-Term Goals

Setting long-term goals is often seen as a daunting task, particularly when you're focused on launching a quick-turnaround million-dollar business. However, achieving substantial success requires vision, foresight, and an unwavering commitment to long-term planning. Think of long-term goals as the North Star that guides your entrepreneurial journey. They ensure you remain focused, aligned, and motivated even when the road gets rocky.

Your long-term goals serve multiple purposes. They're the big-picture outcomes that drive daily actions and decisions. Without them, you can easily get sidetracked by short-term issues or opportunities that don't align with your grand vision. So, let's break down how you can set long-term goals that are both impactful and achievable.

Firstly, take time to understand what success means to you. It's essential to define your ultimate objectives in both quantitative and qualitative terms. Do you aspire to make a set amount of revenue? Or is it more about creating a brand that resonates deeply with your audience? Understand what drives you, and let that fuel your long-term goals.

Next, envision your business in 5, 10, or even 20 years. While immediate wins are exhilarating, thinking far ahead allows you to anticipate industry shifts, evolving customer expectations, and technological advancements. This is critical for sustainable growth. For instance, a long-term goal might be to transform your initial business idea into a global brand or diversify your product range.

Once you've identified your major long-term objectives, break them down into manageable milestones. Each milestone should be a step that brings you closer to your overarching goal. For instance, if you aim to generate $10 million in annual revenue, your first milestone might be to hit $1 million within the first year. Achieving these smaller targets will boost your confidence and keep your momentum going.

Moreover, it's important to make your goals S.M.A.R.T. - Specific, Measurable, Achievable, Relevant, and Time-bound. Setting vague goals like "I want to be successful" won't get you far. Instead, aim for clarity: "I want to achieve a 30% market share in the organic skincare sector within five years." This approach offers you a clear target and a timeline, making it easier to map out the steps needed to get there.

In addition to financial targets, consider goals that enhance your business's intrinsic value. Think about market positioning, brand equity, and customer loyalty. Long-term goals like becoming the go-to brand in your industry or achieving a net promoter score (NPS) of 70 can propel your business into a market leader's position.

It's also crucial to incorporate adaptability into your long-term plans. The business world is ever-changing. Economic fluctuations, technological disruptions, and consumer behavior shifts can all impact your initial plans.

Stay aware of external factors and be ready to pivot your strategy without losing sight of your ultimate goals. Adaptability doesn't mean a lack of direction; rather, it ensures your goals remain relevant and achievable.

As you work towards your long-term goals, constantly measure your progress and recalibrate as necessary. Setting key performance indicators (KPIs) for each milestone will allow you to track how well you're progressing towards your ultimate aims. Regularly review and reassess these KPIs to ensure they remain aligned with your broader vision.

Another critical aspect is involving your team in your long-term vision. Share your goals with them and make sure they understand how their roles contribute to these objectives. When everyone in your organization is working towards the same long-term goals, the synergy can significantly amplify your efforts. It fosters a culture of unity and shared purpose, essential for overcoming inevitable challenges.

Additionally, seek mentorship and advice from those who've tread the path before you. Learning from others' mistakes and successes can provide valuable insights, cutting down your trial and error period. A mentor can offer a fresh perspective, helping you to see potential pitfalls and opportunities you might miss when you're in the weeds of daily operations.

Remember, financial stability is a cornerstone of achieving long-term goals. Proper financial management, including budgeting, forecasting, and maintaining a healthy cash flow, can't be overstated. Ensuring you have the resources to sustain your business during lean times is paramount. This financial prudence allows you to weather storms without derailing your long-term plans.

Moreover, innovation should be a significant component of your long-term strategy. In today's fast-paced world, resting on your laurels can lead to obsolescence. Encourage a culture of innovation where new ideas and improvements are continually sought. This can range from product improvements, operational efficiencies to exploring new markets. Keeping innovation at the core ensures your business remains competitive and relevant.

While setting long-term goals, it's also important to balance ambition with realism. Dream big but ensure your goals are grounded in reality. Overly ambitious targets can be discouraging if they seem unattainable. Conversely, goals that are too easily achieved don't push your boundaries or drive significant growth. Find a balance that challenges you and your team while remaining within the realms of possibility.

Lastly, personal growth and business growth are intertwined. As an entrepreneur, investing in your development is crucial. Continuous learning, whether through formal education, workshops, reading, or networking, keeps you ahead of the curve. Your ability to lead, innovate, and navigate challenges will directly impact your business's ability to achieve long-term success.

In essence, setting long-term goals is about creating a roadmap for your business's future. It involves clear vision, strategic planning, adaptability, team involvement, financial prudence, innovation, balanced ambition, and personal growth. By setting well-defined, thoughtful long-term goals, you not only give your business direction but also inspire your team to strive towards a common purpose. As you embark on your entrepreneurial journey, let these goals be the beacon guiding you towards sustained and meaningful success.

Planning for Sustainable Growth

As we venture down "The Road Ahead," recognizing that winning the immediate battles of setting up and launching a business is just the beginning is essential. Keeping an eye on sustainable growth ensures that your weekend hustle morphs into a thriving enterprise that stands the test of time. So, let's dive into the intricacies of planning for sustained scaling, because growth without groundwork is just a fleeting spark.

First, let's talk about the importance of vision. A clear, long-term vision acts as your North Star, guiding every decision you make and step you take. You might have crushed your 48-hour hustle challenge, but the reality is business landscapes change, and having a lighthouse in the distance keeps your ship from straying off course. Crafting a vision doesn't mean getting lost in abstraction; it means setting tangible milestones that align with your ultimate goal. Whether that's revenue targets, market expansion, or innovation in your product line, these milestones keep you on track and motivated.

Next, there's the significant aspect of financial prudence, which can't be overstated. When revenue starts to flow, the temptation to scale rapidly is strong, but reckless financial decisions can clip your wings just as fast. Sustainable growth isn't about how fast you can expand; it's about how smart you can handle your resources. Reinforce your financial strategy by forecasting future revenues and costs, exploring various funding options judiciously, and maintaining a reserve for unexpected downturns. A solid financial plan gives you the bandwidth to take calculated risks without jeopardizing the whole ship.

Equally important is understanding and leveraging market dynamics. Entrepreneurs often focus intensely on their internal operations, forgetting that external factors can dramatically affect their game plan. Keep your ear to the ground and stay abreast of market trends, consumer behavior, and even regulatory changes. These insights enable you to be proactive rather than reactive, adjusting your strategies in real time to meet market demands and outwit competitors.

Building a robust team is another cornerstone of sustainable growth. Your initial hustle might have been a solo ride or a tight-knit team's effort, but scaling necessitates diversification of skills and expertise. Recruitment should be more than just filling roles; it should aim to build a culture aligned with your vision. Invest in talent that not only brings new skills but also enhances the collective capability of your team. Moreover, leadership is critical—create a hierarchy that empowers employees, fosters innovation, and, most importantly, sustains morale even during challenging phases.

Don't underestimate the power of technology in scaling your operations. Automation, data analytics, and digital marketing aren't just buzzwords; they are enablers of efficiency and growth. Streamlining processes with technology reduces redundant tasks, allowing you and your team to focus on strategy and innovation. However, the tech landscape is ever-evolving, making it imperative to continually update your tech stack and train your team to leverage these tools effectively.

Customer loyalty is another pillar of sustainable growth. Acquiring a customer is just the first step—the real victory lies in retaining them. Building loyalty programs, offering exceptional customer service, and constantly engaging with your customers ensure they return and bring friends along. Remember, a satisfied customer is your best marketer. The feedback loop here is crucial; listen to your customers, iterate based on their inputs, and create a community around your brand.

Sustainability isn't just a business buzzword; it's a necessity. Thinking long-term also means embracing environmentally and socially responsible practices. As consumers become increasingly conscious, aligning your business practices with sustainable values can be a unique selling proposition. Evaluate your supply chain, opt for eco-friendly materials, and highlight social responsibility initiatives. Not only does this contribute to a better world, but it also resonates deeply with a growing segment of the market that values sustainability.

Diversification can act as your safety net. Relying on a single product or market is risky; diversifying your offerings and exploring new markets can cushion against market volatility. Assess complementary products or services that fit naturally with your existing portfolio. This not only spreads the risk but also opens up additional revenue streams. For instance, if your initial product is a hit, think about what ancillary products or upgrades can be introduced to keep the customer engaged and the cash flow steady.

Lastly, always be in the loop of continuous improvement. Sustainable growth involves a commitment to perpetual learning and adaptation. Regularly measure your performance through key performance indicators (KPIs), gather feedback from customers and employees, and be ready to pivot based on insights. The agile mindset, where you can iterate and evolve quickly, will be your most formidable tool in an ever-changing business landscape.

By integrating these strategies, you're not just planning for growth; you're planning for sustained, strategic success. Think of sustainable growth as a marathon—a series of strategic sprints, carefully measured and executed. The road ahead is long and winding, but with these principles as your foundation, every obstacle becomes an opportunity, and every challenge a stepping stone toward your ultimate vision.

Conclusion

As we bring this journey to a close, it's essential to reflect on what we've uncovered about launching a million-dollar business in just 48 hours. Throughout this book, we've delved into the mindset, strategies, and tactical steps required to turn a budding idea into a profitable venture rapidly. But beyond the technical know-how, it's the underlying principles and lessons that will truly propel your success.

The first takeaway is that time, while often perceived as a constraint, can be your greatest ally. The sense of urgency that comes with a 48-hour deadline pushes you to focus on what's essential and discard what's not. It compels you to make swift decisions, test ideas quickly, and iterate based on real-time feedback. Embracing this rapid approach isn't just about working faster; it's about working smarter and more efficiently. It's a practice that, if adopted consistently, can lead to incredible productivity gains.

Another crucial lesson from this book is the importance of mindset. Your attitude towards entrepreneurship can significantly impact your outcomes. A million-dollar mindset isn't about financial ambition alone; it's about resilience, adaptability, and an unwavering belief in your vision. Overcoming fear and doubt is central to this journey. Every entrepreneur faces obstacles, but those who succeed are the ones who view challenges as opportunities to learn and grow.

We've explored various facets of building a strong foundation for your business, from identifying market gaps to knowing your audience, analyzing competition, and setting up your operations. Each step is a piece of a larger puzzle, contributing to the overall success of your venture. A well-researched and meticulously prepared business plan provides direction and clarity, guiding you through the crucial early stages and beyond.

A significant emphasis was placed on the importance of branding and digital presence. In today's interconnected world, building a strong brand identity and an engaging online presence is non-negotiable. Your brand is not just your business's face; it's its soul. It tells your story, connects with your audience on an emotional level, and differentiates you from competitors. Consistent branding and an effective social media strategy can turn casual visitors into loyal customers.

Funding, though often seen as a hurdle, can be navigated through creativity and resourcefulness. Whether you opt for bootstrapping, seeking investors, or exploring alternative financing options, what's crucial is understanding your financial needs and planning accordingly. A strong financial foundation ensures that your business can scale sustainably without compromising on its core values or operational efficiency.

The journey of entrepreneurship is undeniably demanding, but it also offers unparalleled rewards. The ability to create, innovate, and make a significant impact drives many entrepreneurs. It's a path filled with continuous learning, personal growth, and the satisfaction of building something from the ground up. Along the way, managing stress and maintaining work-life balance are vital for long-term success and well-being.

Scaling your operations requires a strategic approach. Streamlining processes, leveraging technology, and building a strong team are key factors that contribute to sustainable growth. Delegation and outsourcing enable you to focus on strategic decisions while ensuring operational efficiency. As your business grows, so do your responsibilities, and having a reliable team can make all the difference.

One of the most rewarding aspects of entrepreneurship is building a loyal customer base. Exceptional customer service and effective loyalty programs foster long-term relationships with your customers. Retaining customers is often more cost-effective than acquiring new ones, and satisfied customers become ambassadors for your brand, driving word-of-mouth referrals.

Continuous improvement and adaptation to market changes are vital for

CONCLUSION

staying competitive. Analyzing performance metrics, seeking feedback, and being open to innovation keep your business agile and responsive. The entrepreneurial landscape is ever-evolving, and those who thrive are those who remain adaptable and open to new ideas.

Networking and strategic partnerships can amplify your reach and drive growth. Building relationships with other entrepreneurs, industry leaders, and potential collaborators opens doors to new opportunities. These connections can provide valuable insights, resources, and support, helping your business navigate challenges and seize opportunities.

As you embark on your entrepreneurial journey, remember that success doesn't occur in isolation. It's the cumulative result of knowledge, effort, resilience, and collaboration. Each step you take, no matter how small it may seem, contributes to your larger vision.

The road ahead is filled with possibilities. Setting long-term goals and planning for sustainable growth ensures that your business continues to thrive. Keep your vision clear, stay committed to your goals, and don't be afraid to take calculated risks. The entrepreneurial journey is a marathon with sprints along the way, and your dedication will propel you forward.

In conclusion, launching a million-dollar business in 48 hours is about more than just quick wins. It's about laying a solid foundation, adopting a growth-oriented mindset, and continuously striving for excellence. With the right blend of passion, resilience, and strategic planning, you can transform your entrepreneurial dreams into a thriving reality. So, go forth, take action, and turn your vision into a million-dollar success story.

Appendix A: Resources and Tools

As you embark on your journey to create a million-dollar business in just 48 hours, having access to the right resources and tools can be a game-changer. This appendix aims to provide you with a comprehensive list of recommended books and websites.

Recommended Books and Websites

When starting a business, especially on a tight timeline, leveraging the right resources can make all the difference. Fortunately, there's an abundance of books and websites filled with insights, strategies, and tips that can accelerate your path to success. Below, we've curated a list of essential readings and websites that provide practical guidance, inspire entrepreneurial spirit, and offer actionable steps to help you achieve your business goals.

Books:

- **"The Lean Startup" by Eric Ries** - This book is a must-read for anyone looking to validate business ideas quickly without wasting time and resources. Ries introduces the concept of 'validated learning,' which is particularly useful when you're aiming to launch a business in 48 hours.
- **"Zero to One" by Peter Thiel** - Thiel's insights into building unique businesses that transcend competition are invaluable. His focus on innovation and creating new market spaces can help you think big, even on a short deadline.
- **"Crushing It!" by Gary Vaynerchuk** - Gary Vee shares stories and

strategies from entrepreneurs who have leveraged personal branding and social media to grow their businesses. It's an excellent motivational read for understanding the immense power of digital marketing.
- **"Start with Why" by Simon Sinek** - Understanding your 'why' is crucial in business. Sinek's book helps you identify your core motivations, which can be the driving force behind your entrepreneurial journey.
- **"The 4-Hour Workweek" by Tim Ferriss** - Ferriss provides unconventional strategies for increasing productivity and automating business processes. This book can guide you in creating a scalable business model that thrives with minimal daily input.
- **"Good to Great" by Jim Collins** - Although more focused on long-term growth, this book's principles of what distinguishes great companies can help you set a strong foundation from the start.
- **"Hooked: How to Build Habit-Forming Products" by Nir Eyal** - Eyal's systematic approach to product development will be beneficial when you're creating a product or service designed to engage customers consistently.

Websites:

- *Entrepreneur (entrepreneur.com)* - This comprehensive resource offers articles, tools, and guides on a wide array of topics relevant to budding entrepreneurs. From business planning to marketing strategies, you'll find actionable advice and success stories.
- *Inc. (inc.com)* - With a focus on growth and innovation, Inc. provides detailed articles, interviews, and case studies that can help you understand what it takes to scale a business effectively.
- *Harvard Business Review (hbr.org)* - While some articles are behind a paywall, HBR offers high-quality, research-backed insights into management, leadership, and strategy. Perfect for those wanting to ground their quick decisions in reliable data.
- *SCORE (score.org)* - This invaluable resource offers free, confidential business mentoring along with numerous templates and guides. Their

extensive library of articles can help with everything from crafting a business plan to marketing strategies.
- **Product Hunt (producthunt.com)** - For staying updated on the latest tech tools and products that can give your business an edge, Product Hunt is essential. It's also a great place to launch your product and get early user feedback.
- **HubSpot Blog (blog.hubspot.com)** - HubSpot delivers in-depth guides on sales, marketing, and customer retention strategies. Their templates and tool recommendations can streamline your initial setup process.
- **NerdWallet (nerdwallet.com)** - When you're looking at financing options, NerdWallet offers comparisons and reviews of various loan products, credit cards, and other financial services tailored for small businesses.
- **Copyblogger (copyblogger.com)** - A fantastic resource for all things content marketing, Copyblogger offers tips and tutorials on creating compelling content that attracts and retains customers.
- **Shopify Blog (shopify.com/blog)** - If you're considering an e-commerce venture, the Shopify Blog provides practical advice on setting up and scaling an online store, along with trends and best practices in online retail.

In addition to these books and websites, it's also beneficial to follow thought leaders in the entrepreneurial space. Tim Ferriss' podcast, "The Tim Ferriss Show", hosts a variety of guests with unique insights into business, productivity, and innovation. Similarly, "How I Built This" by Guy Raz offers compelling stories from entrepreneurs who started with humble beginnings and built empires.

Books like "Tools of Titans" by Tim Ferriss and "The Innovator's Dilemma" by Clayton Christensen, although not strictly about launching quickly, offer deeper insights into effective strategies and frameworks that can provide lasting competitive advantages. It's about getting inspired and informed by those who have walked the path before you.

Moreover, consider joining online communities and forums centered around entrepreneurship. Websites like Reddit (specifically the r/entrepreneur subreddit) and forums such as Indie Hackers provide a platform to ask questions, share experiences, and gain insights from fellow entrepreneurs. Being part of such communities can offer real-time advice and a sense of camaraderie, which is invaluable on the entrepreneurial journey.

Podcast recommendations wouldn't be complete without mentioning "The Smart Passive Income Podcast" by Pat Flynn. Flynn shares insights into creating multiple income streams and passive income opportunities, which align perfectly with the goal of building a business that not only starts quickly but scales efficiently.

Finally, remember to utilize academic and government resources that provide free or low-cost information. Websites like the U.S. Small Business Administration (sba.gov) offer extensive guides and templates for everything from business planning to financing. Similarly, many universities offer free online courses or articles on entrepreneurship, which can be a handy resource when you need to learn something specific quickly.

In summary, the path to creating a million-dollar business within a tight timeframe is undeniably challenging, but with the right resources at your disposal, it becomes significantly more attainable. The books and websites listed here are chosen for their practical, actionable insights and their ability to inspire and guide you through each crucial step of your entrepreneurial journey. Dive into these resources with an open mind and a willingness to adapt and learn, and you'll find yourself well-equipped to conquer the challenges ahead. Remember, knowledge is power, but applied knowledge is what leads to success.

www.ingramcontent.com/pod-product-compliance
Lightning Source LLC
Chambersburg PA
CBHW071208240526
45470CB00018B/1589